A POCKET GUIDE TO THE

WILD
ATLANTIC
WAY

Gill Books
Hume Avenue, Park West, Dublin 12

www.gillbooks.ie

Gill Books is an imprint of M.H. Gill & Co.

Copyright © Teapot Press Ltd 2020

ISBN: 978-0-7171-8600-6

This book was created and produced by Teapot Press Ltd

Text by Fiona Biggs
Designed by Tony Potter & Becca Wildman

Printed in EU

This book is typeset in Garamond & Dax

A CIP catalogue record for this book is available
from the British Library.

5 4 3 2 1

A POCKET GUIDE TO THE

WILD ATLANTIC WAY

FIONA BIGGS

Gill Books

Contents

Introduction

The Wild Atlantic Way, *Slí an Atlantaigh Fhiáin,* is a 2,500-kilometre tourist trail that passes through nine counties and three provinces, from Kinsale on the southern Celtic Sea coast, around the whole of the Atlantic coast to the border between Donegal and Derry. The Wild Atlantic Way is an important part of the work of Fáilte Ireland, the national tourism development authority, and was officially launched in 2014 by Minister of State for Tourism and Sport, Michael Ring.

The route is broken down into stages (see page 8); along the route there are 15 Signature Discovery Points, 157 Discovery Points, around 1,000 attractions and over 2,500 activities.

You can follow the route in any direction, taking in just a small section, or making a longer trip depending on your interests and the time available. One thing is certain: you will encounter some of the most beautiful scenery in the world, and gain an insight into over 5,000 years of Ireland's fascinating history.

The 15 Signature
Discovery Points of
the Wild Atlantic Way

Malin Head
Fanad Head

DONEGAL

DERRY

ANTRIM

Slieve League

TYRONE

Mullaghmore Head

Downpatrick Head

FERMANAGH

ARMAGH

DOWN

MONAGHAN

SLIGO

Keem
Strand

MAYO

LEITRIM

CAVAN

Irish
Sea

ROSCOMMON

LONGFORD

LOUTH

Killary Harbour

MEATH

Derrigimlagh

WESTMEATH

Atlantic
Ocean

GALWAY

OFFALY

KILDARE

DUBLIN

Cliffs of
Moher

CLARE

LAOIS

WICKLOW

Loop
Head

LIMERICK

TIPPERARY

CARLOW

KILKENNY

WEXFORD

Blaskets
View

WATERFORD

Skelligs
Viewpoint

KERRY

CORK

Counties
of the Wild
Atlantic Way

Dursey
Island

Old Head of
Kinsale

Celtic Sea

Mizen Head

This book divides the Wild Atlantic Way into several stages, as follows:

The Southwest (Counties Cork & Kerry)
Stages of the Southwest are:

West Cork: Kinsale to Mizen Head
Sheep's Head & Beara Peninsulas: Durrus to Tuosist
Iveragh Peninsula: Kenmare to Killorglin

The Midwest (Counties Kerry, Limerick & Clare)
Stages of the Midwest are:

Dingle Peninsula & the Shannon Estuary: Dingle to Carrigafoyle Castle
The Cliff Coast: Glin to The Burren

The West (Counties Galway & Mayo)
Stages of the West are:

The Connemara Coast: Galway to Killary Harbour
The Mayo Coast: Aasleagh Falls to Erris Head

The Northwest (Counties Sligo, Leitrim & Donegal)
Stages of the Northwest are:

The Surf Coast: Enniscrone to Mullaghmore
The North-West Headlands: Donegal Bay to Bunbeg
The Northern Peninsulas: Bloody Foreland to Malin Head

The entire route is well signposted with the Wild Atlantic Way logo. There are also steel signs for Signature Discovery Points and Discovery Points. Signature Discovery points are highlighted in the book like this: *Dursey Island.* Discovery points are highlighted like this: *Timoleague*

Check online for the opening times of the attractions described in the book, as these are subject to change.

Caution: Beaches can be dangerous and terrain can be difficult; always heed any warning notices.

Signposts
Look out for the distinctive Wild Atlantic Way directional signs.

Discovery Points
These have very distinctive corten steel signs, often accompanied by information boards.

Mizen Head

CHAPTER 1 Kinsale to Mizen Head

What to look out for along the way.

Kinsale to Clonakilty

Key towns and villages
Kinsale
Timoleague
Courtmacsherry
Clonakilty

Beaches
Harbour View Beach; Sandycove;
Garrylucas; Garrettstown;
Broadstrand; Inchydoney; Seven
Heads Bay; Dunworly

Monuments
Desmond Castle; Charles Fort;
James Fort; Ringrone Castle;
Timoleague Friary

Gardens
Lisselan Gardens, Clonakilty

Walk
Old Head of Kinsale Loop

Food and Drink
A Taste of West Cork Food Festival
(September); Kinsale Gourmet
Festival (October)

Don't Miss!
The Old Head of Kinsale; The
International Museum of Wine;
birdwatching; surfing

Clonakilty to Skibbereen

Key towns and villages
Rosscarbery
Castletownshend
Skibbereen

Viewing point
Toe Head

Beaches
Tragumna; Red Strand;
Long Strand; Owenahincha;
Rosscarbery

Monuments
Bohonagh Stone Circle;
Coppinger's Court; Drombeg
Stone Circle; Gurranes Stone
Row (the Three Fingers);
Knockdrum Fort; the Michael
Collins House

Gardens
Liss Ard Estate; Drishane House
and Garden; Inish Beg

Offshore island
Inish Beg Island

Don't Miss!
Whale- and dolphin-watching;
Rineen Woods; The Sky Garden;
Lough Hyne Visitor Centre

Baltimore to Mizen Head

Key towns and villages
Baltimore
Schull
Ballydehob

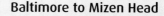

Viewing points
Mizen Head; Brow Head;
Dundeady Headland

Monuments
Baltimore Castle; Baltimore
Beacon; Sherkin Monastery;
Toormore Altar Wedge Tomb;
Dunlough Castle

Beach
Barleycove

Offshore islands
Sherkin Island; Heir Island; Cape
Clear

Festivals
Ballydehob Jazz Fest; Trad Fest;
Country Music Fest; Folk Fest;
Boat Gathering

Don't Miss!
The Fastnet Rock; The Teardrop
of Ireland; Schull Harbour;
Cunnamore Pier; Lough Hyne;
Baltimore Harbour

The southern starting point of the Wild Atlantic Way is the pretty Irish Heritage Town of Kinsale, which developed from a simple medieval fishing village to a substantial garrison town. You'll find plenty to see and do (and eat – it's become something of a gourmet destination) before you set off westwards.

The town hosts a number of festivals throughout the year: the Kinsale Regatta (first weekend in August), the Kinsale Arts

Kinsale
The quaint yachting harbour of Kinsale is one of many colourful gems strung along the coastline of County Cork.

Weekend in July and the Kinsale Gourmet Festival in October. It is one of the many hosting locations for the annual A Taste of West Cork Food Festival in September.

RMS *Lusitania*, hit by torpedoes.

Historically, Kinsale was the site of the famous Battle of Kinsale in 1601, and of the sinking by a German U-boat of a British passenger ship, RMS *Lusitania*, in May 1915, when 1,195 civilian passengers died. Those who died on

Ringrone Castle.

the *Lusitania* were buried in the graveyard attached to the ancient St Multose Church.

Kinsale is an easy town to walk around, so take a bit of time to visit the Kinsale Museum and Desmond Castle, with its fascinating International Museum of Wine. A few kilometres south of the town is Ringrone Castle, a 13th-century tower house built on the River Bandon to defend the bay. It was almost completely destroyed during the Battle of Kinsale and only a fragment remains, but is worth a visit for the panoramic views.

A 30–40-minute walk from the harbour (follow the

Charles Fort
Overlooking Kinsale Bay. The star shape is visible clearly from the air.

signs for the Scilly Walk/Charles Fort) is Charles Fort, an impressive and well-preserved star-shaped fort built at the end of the 18th century, during the reign of King Charles II. The fort played a significant role in some of the key events of Irish history. The views over the water are spectacular. Almost directly across the estuary is the earlier James Fort, built to defend the harbour at the beginning of the 17th century, during the reign of King James I. The pentagonal fort commands views of the river, harbour and town. Sandycove, a small sheltered bay that is popular with serious swimmers, is just a short walk from the fort.

If you feel like stretching your legs, the ***Old Head of Kinsale Loop*** (six kilometres) is worth the effort. You can't get right to the end of the cliff-flanked headland as a private golf course has been built at the tip, but the views are spectacular nonetheless. Garrylucas (Garrettstown Beach/White Strand) is a Blue Flag beach that is popular with swimmers and surfers.

As you head towards *Timoleague*, you'll pass the pristine sands of Harbour View Beach. Timoleague is a typical small Irish village built around a fine 13th-century Franciscan friary overlooking Courtmacsherry Bay. It's an area that is renowned for birdwatching, especially at low tide.

The next stop on the route is Courtmacsherry, a picturesque seaside village with a sheltered sandy beach. There's a lovely woodland walk from the car park at the beach – go in May when the bluebells are in flower. Continue through the woods to Wood Point for a bird's-eye view of the ***Old Head of Kinsale***.

The Old Head of Kinsale.

En route to Seven Heads Bay you'll pass Broadstrand, a long, sheltered sand and pebble beach. The two beaches at Dunworly are also popular.

Clonakilty, renowned for its award-winning black pudding, is a sizeable seaside town situated on Clonakilty Bay.

Clonakilty Bay

The Blue Flag beach at Inchydoney is a surfing destination and one of West Cork's most family-friendly beaches. The Michael Collins House is worth a visit, as are the beautiful Lisselan Gardens, a 12-hectare homage to the Irish gardener and landscape designer William Robinson (1838–1935), an early proponent of the wild garden – he popularised the English cottage garden, beloved of gardeners to this day.

Along this stretch of the coast there are lots of tiny coves and beaches. *Inchydoney* Island, just south of Clonakilty and connected to the mainland by two causeways, has two beaches, one of which has been awarded a Blue Flag. Red Strand, near Rosscarbery, is good for surfing. Long Strand is stunning but unsuitable for swimming. Owenahincha is a popular beach, connected via a short cliff path to the Blue Flag Rosscarbery beach. This part of the coast is a haven for whales, dolphins and a huge variety of seabirds.

Michael Collins
The revolutionary, soldier and politician was a leading figure in the early 20th-century struggle for Irish independence from Britain.

Bohonagh
Winter solstice
sunset on 21
December.

Drombeg
A perfect stone
circle overlooking
the sea.

Travelling west from Clonakilty, just outside Rosscarbery (home to Ireland's smallest cathedral, St Fachtna's) you will come across Bohonagh stone circle, dating from the Early Bronze Age, and Coppinger's Court, a substantial fortified house built in the early 16th century. A little further on, Drombeg, one of Ireland's best examples of a stone circle, is sited in a beautiful setting. The 'Druid's Altar', the only horizontal stone in the circle, was positioned to align with the winter solstice sunset on 21 December. The Drombeg stone circle is all that is still standing of a Bronze Age settlement, although the foundations of habitations have been uncovered there.

Dundeady headland, the site of *Galley Head* lighthouse, which dates from 1875 and is still active, offers panoramic views. There is no general access to the lighthouse compound, which has been meticulously renovated as tourist accommodation.

Galley Head lighthouse.

Harry Clarke
A detail from one of the Harry Clarke windows at St Barrahane's Church, Castletownshend. Clarke was a leading figure in the Arts and Crafts movement, producing stunning stained glass and book illustrations in the early 20th century.

Castletownshend, perched on the north side of Castlehaven harbour, is a picture-postcard village built around the castle that gave it its name. It's worth stopping here to explore the village and the surrounding area. The village church, St Barrahane's, high on a hill above the village, has three beautiful stained-glass windows by Harry Clarke.

A short distance from the village is the extraordinary Gurrane's Stone Row, also known as the Three Fingers, a series of three tall standing stones (originally five) that

The Three Fingers
Bronze Age standing stones.

Wild Atlantic Way
Sign for Toe Head.

have remained in position since the Bronze Age. Close by is Knockdrum, a partially restored early medieval stone cashel, or fort, with lovely views out to sea. *Toe Head,* with its strange rock formations, is a dramatic cliffside viewing point over Atlantic. It is close to the Blue Flag beach of Tragumna.

Drishane House, built by Thomas Somerville in the late 18th century and occupied by the Somerville family for 250 years, was home to Edith Somerville and her cousin Violet Martin, better known as Somerville and Ross, authors of *The Experiences of an Irish R.M.* Drishane is a lovely example of a small Georgian country house and is open to the public in the summer, as are its gardens.

The Teardrop of Ireland

Sea conditions permitting, you can take a boat trip around the Fastnet Rock, the most southerly land point in Ireland and home to a lighthouse that is widely regarded as an astonishing feat of engineering. Fastnet became known as 'The Teardrop of Ireland' – it was the last sight of Ireland for many emigrants to the United States during and after the Great Famine.

Construction of the first lighthouse was begun in 1853; it was replaced in 1904.

Emigration
During the Great Famine (An Gorta Mór) of 1845–49, over a million people in Ireland died and a further million emigrated.

Violet Martin
Edith Somerville made this portrait of her cousin, the author Violet Martin, in her riding habit at the start of what became a lifelong friendship. Begun on 27 February 1886, it was painted at Drishane House.

Travelling in the direction of Skibbereen, take the turn-off for Union Hall village and follow the road out of town to Rineen Woods. A magical place for a leisurely circular stroll and a picnic, its individually crafted fairy houses (installed and maintained by a local artist) make it a great destination for young families.

Back on the road to Skibbereen, stop off at Liss Ard Estate and Gardens. The house has been turned into a hotel, and in the summer the beautiful gardens are open to the public. The 163-acre site includes woodland, a wildflower meadow, a water

Drishane House.

garden and the unique Sky Garden, designed as a naked-eye observatory.

Skibbereen is a busy town, host to the annual Skibbereen Arts Festival in July/August, with national and international music, film, dance and theatre. It's followed a few days later by the three-day Skibbereen History Festival, with a packed agenda of lectures, discussions, films and field trips. The Heritage Centre on Upper Bridge Street houses a permanent exhibition dealing with the Great Famine of the mid-19th century, documenting events in this notoriously badly affected area. On the same street, the *Lough Hyne* Visitor Centre provides an introduction to the unusual saltwater lake in the marine nature reserve just south of the town.

The small town of Baltimore, built around a pretty natural harbour, has a somewhat turbulent past. Over the centuries it was frequently invaded by pirates. These days it's a popular summer destination with lots to see and do, including deep sea fishing, whale and dolphin watching, sailing and diving. The ragged coastline around Baltimore is formed by Carbery's Hundred Isles, among which are several inhabited offshore islands, including *Heir Island, Sherkin Island* (with the remains of a Franciscan abbey and an O'Driscoll castle) and *Cape Clear* (renowned internationally for its Bird Observatory), all of which are just a short ferry trip from *Baltimore Harbour*. Inish Beg, a private island, has beautiful gardens that are open to the public throughout the year.

Must-sees in Baltimore are Baltimore Castle and the Baltimore Beacon (at opposite ends of the town). The

Baltimore from the air.

castle's Irish name – Dún na Séad (the jewel fort) – puts a romantic gloss on the tax-collecting activities of its owners. The Baltimore Beacon was built after the 1798 Rebellion just beyond the western limit of the town as a marker for passing ships. It is a popular viewing point for the nearer offshore islands.

Every May Baltimore hosts a traditional music festival, the Baltimore Fiddle Fair, offering lively sessions, a historical walking tour of the town and a musical cruise. The same month sees the Baltimore Wooden Boat Festival, a celebration of the town's long and proud tradition of wooden boatbuilding. It coincides with the weekend of the Baltimore Seafood Festival.

Along the road from Baltimore to Ballydehob you'll pass *Cunnamore Pier*, another ferry embarkation

The Baltimore Beacon.

Ballydehob's 12-arched bridge.

point for Heir and Sherkin Islands. A magnificent 12-arched railway bridge dominates the landscape around Ballydehob, a small former mining town with a big reputation for music and the arts – the Trad Fest in April is followed by the Jazz Fest in May and the Country Music and Folk Fests in June. The week-long Summer Fest in August incorporates the annual Boat Gathering, and there is also a Theatre Fest every August. The Old-Time Threshing and Vintage Festival in October is a lively and fun-filled celebration of Ballydehob's agricultural past and present.

The last town on the way to *Mizen Head* at the tip of the Mizen Peninsula is Schull (pronounced 'skull', but less gruesome than it sounds – the name comes from the Irish word for 'school'; it was once believed that the town was built on a medieval monastic school). It's a lively place, particularly in the summer, with lots of interesting shops selling locally produced goods. The Schull Country Market, held every Sunday from late spring until early autumn, showcases local crafts and food products.

Schull
Small boats anchored at Schull.

Travelling west from Schull to the last point on this section of the Wild Atlantic Way, *Mizen Head*, you will pass the Toormore altar wedge tomb, believed to date from the Iron Age. It is said to have been used as a Mass rock during Penal times, when Catholics were forbidden to say or attend Mass.

Crookhaven Lighthouse on Rock Island (a promontory rather than an island, despite its name), was built in 1843 in the most south-westerly parish in Ireland, after the loss of a number of ships in Crookhaven Harbour. The living quarters, now in private ownership, were extended and renovated between 1999 and 2008 and are now rented out as luxury holiday accommodation.

Brow Head, the Irish mainland's southernmost point, has panoramic views; there is an early 19th-century signal tower at its highest point. The views are worth the hike. This windswept craggy spot, with its caves and disused mineshafts, was used as a film location in *Star Wars: The Last Jedi* (2017).

A little to the north of Brow Head is a lovely sheltered beach, Barleycove. This Blue Flag beach is popular for both swimming and surfing.

A short drive through spectacular scenery will bring you to the vertiginous cliffs of *Mizen Head* at Ireland's south-western tip. The visitor centre is open every day from the middle of March to November; since 2011 the lighthouse has been accessible via a sturdy footbridge.

Brow Head
Ireland's southernmost point.

Dunlough Castle, originally one of Ireland's oldest Norman castles, was built to take advantage of the wide view of the Atlantic. The existing structure is believed to date from the late 15th or early 16th century. Its location at the top of

Dunlough Castle

the Mizen Peninsula is now known as Three Castle Head – a reference to the fact that three of the castle's original towers are still standing.

Durrus River

What to look out for along the way.

Key towns and villages
Durrus
Bantry
Glengarriff
Castletownbere
Allihies
Eyeries
Kenmare

Viewing Points
Firkeel Bay; Dursey Sound;
Ballydonegan Bay; Ardacluggin;
Ring of Beara; Ardea Castle;
Coomakesta Pass; Ring of Kerry;
Ballinskelligs Bay; Bolus Head;
Coomanaspig Pass; Kerry Cliffs

Monuments
Kilnaruane Stone; Kealkill Stone
Circle; Kildreelig; Hag of Beara;
Carriganass Castle; Dunboy
Castle; Ardea Castle

Gardens
Garnish Island; Derreen Gardens; Kilvarock Garden; Garra Fado Garden; Bantry House and Gardens; The Ewe Experience Sculpture Gardens; Mill Cove Sculpture Gardens; Glengarriff Bamboo Park; Carraig Abhainn Gardens

Walks
Sheep's Head; Lighthouse Loop; Glengarriff Nature Reserve Loop; Gleninchaquin; Bere Island Loops; Dursey Island Loop

Offshore Islands
Bere Island; Whiddy Island; Garnish Island; Dursey Island; Abbey Island; Skelligs; Seal Island

Festivals
West Cork Literary Festival, Bantry (July); Festival of the Sea, Castletownbere (August); Eyeries Family Festival (July); Ballydehob Summer Fest (August); the Old-Time Threshing and Vintage Festival, Ballydehob (October)

Music
West Cork Chamber Music Festival, Bantry (June/July); Masters of Tradition, Bantry (August)

Don't Miss!
Seal Island
Gleninchaquin Waterfall
Dursey Island Cable Car
Allihies Copper Mine Museum
A Grand Day Out
Puxley Manor
The Dereenies

Sheep's Head
The lighthouse at Sheep's Head.

Straddling the Mizen and *Sheep's Head* Peninsulas, the attractive little village of Durrus is a good stopping point on the Wild Atlantic Way. While there are established routes for serious walkers, you can take a gentle stroll around the 1.7-acre Kilvarock Garden with its sweeping views over Bantry Bay and Dunmanus Bay. The garden's micro-climate accommodates a wide range of exotic shrubs and trees in the different zones.

You can enjoy spectacular views by driving almost to the tip of the Sheep's Head Peninsula, where a small lighthouse warns sailors about the rocky cliffs.

A short (4-kilometre) loop walk will take you from the car park to the lighthouse and back again. If you feel like hiking to the top of *Mount Seefin* you will be rewarded with panoramic views over the surrounding countryside.

Mount Seefin

Sheep's Head seen from Seefin Viewpoint. Enshrined in legend as one of Fionn Mac Cumhaill's lookouts.

Carraig Abhainn Gardens covers 2.5 acres in a woodland setting in the middle of Durrus village. On the West Cork Garden Trail, it's host to a wide variety of rare plants, all carefully chosen to take advantage of the sheltered climate of the garden. Dotted with statues and other sculptures along the self-guided walks, Carraig Abhainn is a tranquil and relaxing place to while away a couple of hours. It's open on weekdays from March to October (Sundays by appointment only).

Carraig Abhainn Gardens
Lose yourself in this lush garden for a few hours.

Bantry, 34 kilometres east of Sheep's Head, is a colourful harbour town that nestles comfortably in the surrounding landscape. The gateway to the Beara Peninsula, it developed from an ancient settlement, and is named after one of King Conor Mac Nessa's sons. People were probably drawn to the place because of its wonderful natural harbour.

Bantry is a lively place in the summer months, with the West Cork Chamber Music Festival in June/July, the West Cork Literary Festival in July, and Masters of Tradition in August. Every September the people of Bantry are enthusiastic participants in the Taste of West Cork Food Festival.

Bantry Harbour
One of the deepest natural harbours in Europe.

Whiddy Island
This tranquil island has a three-hour waymarked walk.

The Chamber Music Festival is hosted in Bantry House, a fine stately home dating from the early 18th century (with sympathetic 19th-century additions), with wonderful views across the bay to *Whiddy Island*. The house and its beautiful Italianate gardens are open to the public.

Sparsely populated Whiddy Island is a 10–15-minute ferry ride from *Bantry Pier*. It's a bird-watchers' paradise, and the island can be walked in around three hours. You can hire bikes there if you prefer to cycle. Some of the West Cork Literary Festival events take place here in July, but it is usually a very tranquil place, with just one pub. The ferry runs up to six times a day throughout the year.

Bantry House

This stately home is still owned by the descendants of its builder, the Earl of Bantry.

Wolfe Tone

This statue in Bantry commemorates his role as leader of the 1798 Rebellion.

Just outside Bantry is the Kilnaruane Stone, a magnificent remnant of a monastic foundation. The carvings on one side of the stone are believed to depict the Brendan Voyage, and locals refer to the stone as St Brendan's Stone for this reason.

Leaving Bantry and heading north towards Glengarriff, take a right turn at Ballylickey and follow the road to Kealkill stone circle, with its commanding views of the bay. Carriganass Castle, now a fairly substantial ruin, was built by the O'Sullivan Beare family in the middle of the 16th century.

Kilnaruane Stone

The Beara peninsula is renowned for its craggy shoreline and rugged landscape. The small seaside town of Glengarriff (meaning 'rough glen') at the entry point to the peninsula is a popular tourist destination.

Although beaches on the peninsula are few and far between, there are some easy swimming places, such as the Blue Pool, just outside town. The Ring of Beara, a 200-kilometre scenic road, intersects with the Wild Atlantic Way along most of the Beara Peninsula, including Bere Island and Dursey Island.

Glengarriff
The gateway to the Beara Peninsula.

A Grand Day Out

Remember those Sunday drives where you didn't really have a destination in mind, but just stopped where the fancy took you? A Grand Day Out uses red fish signs to point you towards the many attractions of the Beara peninsula, ranging from art galleries to water sports, and

Kenmare Bay

Red fish logo
This was designed
by the award-
winning ceramic
artist Gráinne Watts.

everything of interest in between, including great food
opportunities. At the end of the day you can say you've had
'a grand day out' on the beautiful peninsula on the south-
west coast of Ireland, lying between Kenmare Bay to the

Garnish Island
The Italian tea house.

Martello Tower
Garnish Island.

From March to October you can take a ferry from Glengarriff's main pier to *Garnish Island* (Ilnacullin), just off the coast. When the island was privately owned by the Bryce family a unique garden was created. The mild climate makes it possible to maintain the wonderfully lush garden, which has a number of unexpected buildings, including a clock tower and a Grecian temple. The landscaping incorporates a miniature Italian garden with a tea house. The island is also home to one of the Martello towers that were built as defensive look-outs during the Napoleonic Wars.

Garnish is now in state ownership. On your way to the island, keep your eyes open for Seal Island, home to a large colony of harbour seals.

Another unique Glengarriff garden is the Bamboo Park, created by a French couple in 1999. Although the focus of this lush garden is fast-growing bamboo, it is also home to a large collection of ferns and palm trees.

Just outside Glengarriff on the road to Kenmare is Glengarriff Nature Reserve, which contains some of Ireland's last remaining natural woodland. The warm moist micro-climate of the area means that it is, in effect, a rainforest. It's a haven for wildlife and a great place for a walk – five short walks are signposted, and they can be combined to make a loop.

Bamboo Park
The mild climate lends itself to exotic planting.

Just up the road from Glengarriff Nature Reserve, the Ewe Experience Sculpture Garden is well worth a small detour. An award-winning interactive nature and art experience that will appeal to all ages, the Ewe has four gardens – Falling Water, Timeless Glen, Environmental Forest and Valley of Eden. A private garden, open to the public from 1 June to 1 September, it is a wonderful combination of art, nature, humour and whimsy. Allow up to two hours to see the whole garden.

Coming back to the route, Castletownbere is an important fishing port located on Berehaven Harbour. Like all of the Beara Peninsula, the harbour was in the territory of the O'Sullivan Beres – the remains of their stronghold,

Castletownbere

Dunboy Castle
Only the foundations remain.

Dunboy Castle, can be found nearby. The O'Sullivan Beres were well placed to levy taxes on the fishing boats entering the harbour.

Castletownbere's connection to the sea is celebrated every August bank holiday weekend and the week following with an action-packed Festival of the Sea. Many of the events are free, and include a regatta, children's fancy dress parade, gig races, pillow fights and a poker classic night.

Puxley Manor and the Curse of the O'Sullivans

On land adjacent to Dunboy Castle is Puxley Manor, built in the early 1700s by copper tycoons, but seemingly doomed by the curse of the O'Sullivans – the manor was built on O'Sullivan land that became forfeit to the crown after a rebellion in the 17th century.

The Puxleys became poor when the rich reserves of copper became exhausted. They went back to England, leaving the house to be looked after by caretakers. Burned down by the IRA in 1921, the house was sold in 1927 and again in 1999, this time to an investment consortium. A huge refurbishment project was started, but was scuppered by the financial crash of 2008, and the partially restored manor house was abandoned once again, before finally being converted to a hotel.

Puxley Manor
View of the building before restoration.

Bere Island
Martello Tower on Bere Island.

The Sculpture Garden at Mill Cove Gallery in *Castletownbere* has a permanent sculpture exhibition of over 40 works in a 40-acre garden overlooking the sea. It's open from April to September, or by appointment.

This part of the peninsular coastline is dominated by *Bere Island*. The island, now a haven of tranquillity, was heavily fortified during the Napoleonic Wars, when four Martello towers were built. In the early 20th century shipping defences were constructed on the island; the harbour was an important Royal Navy port during the First World War. The island has several fairly short loop walks that give stunning views over the bay. Back on the mainland, travelling east towards Dursey Sound, take some time to enjoy the magnificent views at Firkeel Bay, where steep cliffs drop into the sea. There is a daily car ferry service to Bere Island from Castletownbere.

At the very tip of the Beara Peninsula is *Dursey Island*, which can be reached all year round by Ireland's only cable car and the most reliable form of transport to and from the island. Although it's inhabited, Dursey has no bars or restaurants, so take a picnic. There is a 14-kilometre loop walk around the island that gives views out to the Skelligs and along the coastlines of Kerry and West Cork.

Dursey Island

The cable car was inaugurated in 1969.

If you double back on the road to Dursey and head eastwards towards Allihies, you will pass Ballydonegan Bay, set against a backdrop of mountains. The bay is wild and very beautiful, but has a wonderful sandy beach at Ballydonegan.

Nestled into the peaceful countryside behind Ballydonegan Bay, Allihies is a colourful two-pub village, dominated by one of the engine houses of the Allihies copper mines, established in the early 19th century by John Puxley. It was the first industrial mine in the area, although copper ore had been mined as far back as the Bronze Age. The mine became a huge employer in the area, but the work was dangerous and poorly paid. Most of the mining stopped in 1884 when the copper failed and many of the redundant miners emigrated to Montana in the United States. The full story of the Allihies mines is told in the Allihies Copper Mine Museum, housed in a former Methodist church. A

Ballydonegan Bay

Set in a stunning mountain landscape.

waymarked walking trail will take you past almost all of the engine houses that served the mine. The elevated location provides outstanding views.

A few kilometres to the south west of Eyeries, the rocky coastline at Ardacluggin, with sweeping views to the Beara coast and the Iveragh Peninsula, is home to a variety of wildflowers in season.

Eyeries is a small, friendly village in a stunning location. The annual Eyeries Family Festival, held on the third weekend in July, has something for everyone, from food to music, and from boat races to Irish dancing, with any number of fun family activities in between. You'll find peace and tranquillity at the Garra Fado Garden, a small garden covering just over an acre, which has beautiful displays of the hardy plants that are suited to the challenging salt-laden and windy climate of the peninsula.

The Hag of Beara

Just after leaving Eyeries, follow the road to the Kilcatherine Peninsula and you will come across the Hag of Beara, a large rock that is steeped in legend. It is supposed to be the head of a fairy woman, petrified while she waited for her husband. The Hag features in many legends throughout the country, but her influence was particularly strong in Cork and Kerry. She was said to have been the goddess of winter, growing younger and stronger during that season – her powers diminished as spring melted into summer. It is said that if the weather on St Brigid's Day, 1

February, is bad, the Hag is still asleep and winter will soon come to an end; however, if the day is bright and clear, she's awake, concentrating on making winter last longer. People still leave small tokens for the Hag at the rock.

Lauragh, a tiny village in a stunning location at the head of Kilmackillogue Harbour, is situated on the Cork/Kerry border. The Derreen Gardens, just outside Lauragh, cover an area of about 75 acres, providing a haven for wildlife and a showcase for a variety of exotic plants. The stars of the show, though, are the rhododendrons. The garden, created in 1870 by the fifth Marquess of Lansdowne, was originally much larger, planted with specimen plants from India and Canada. It has several walks through woodland and bamboo groves, with views over Kilmackillogue Harbour and the majestic MacGillicuddy's Reeks. Children will be on the lookout for the Derreenies, the little folk who live in the little houses along the Glade Walk.

One of the last stops before Kenmare and the next stage of the Wild Atlantic Way is the ruin of Ardea Castle, near Tuosist, built in a superbly defensive position overlooking the *Kenmare River*. An O'Sullivan Bere stronghold for four centuries, it was destroyed by Cromwell's troops in the mid-17th century. While there is little left to see, the views are amazing.

Also near Tuosist is Gleninchaquin Park, with an impressive waterfall flowing over the rock face (it's at its most spectacular after a period of heavy rain). The park, which covers several hundred acres, is an area of outstanding natural beauty. There are six designated walks, ranging from easy stroll to challenging hike.

Kenmare River

A summer sunrise over the estuary just below Kenmare.

Kenmare Bay from Sheen Falls

CHAPTER 3 Kenmare to Killorglin

What to look out for along the way.

Key towns and villages
Sneem
Waterville
Portmagee
Cahersiveen
Glenbeigh
Killorglin

Viewing Points
Geokaun Mountain (Valentia Island); Kerry Cliffs; Bray Tower

Beaches
White Strand; Glanbeg Strand; Derrynane Bay; St Finian's Bay (the Glen); Inny Strand; Ballinskelligs Beach; Rossbeigh Beach; Kells Bay

Monuments
Dunboy Castle; Kenmare Stone Circle; Staigue Fort; Derrynane House; Loher Stone Fort; Eightercua; McCarthy Mór Tower; Ballinskelligs Priory; Kildreelig; Cromwell Point Lighthouse; Ballycarbery Castle; Cahergal Stone Fort

Gardens
Glanleam Gardens (Valentia); Kells Bay House and Gardens

Walks
Bray Head Loop Walk; Beentee Loop; Lomanagh Loop; Beentee Head Loop

Offshore Islands
The Skelligs; Valentia Island

Food & Drink
Valentia Island King Scallop Festival (May); Flavour of Killorglin Festival (September)

Music
Cahersiveen Roots Music Festival (May)

Festivals
Puck Fair (August); Sneem Storytelling Festival (November)

Don't Miss!
Puffins (Skellig Michael); Skellig Experience Visitor Centre; Ring of Kerry; The Tetrapod Trackway; Coomakesta Pass; The Sky Walk; Coomanaspig Pass

Linking the Ring of Beara with the Ring of Kerry, Kenmare is on the junction of the Beara and Iveragh Peninsulas. It is surrounded by one of the most unspoilt natural environments in Europe. Whether your focus is the Ring of Kerry or the Wild Atlantic Way, this attractive town is a good base. It's something of a tourist hub, with a large number of pubs, cafés and restaurants for the size of its permanent population. Kenmare is a small town with a big history – its roots go back to the Bronze Age, as evidenced by the Kenmare Stone Circle, the largest stone circle in the south-west of Ireland. Unusually, the circle is located in the town itself and is known locally as 'The

Kenmare Stone Circle
The 13 standing stones encircle a burial boulder.

Seal family

Seals are a frequent sight in Kenmare Bay.

Shrubberies'. The Vikings established a settlement here, known as Ceann Mara, or 'head of the sea'. The modern town was established by the first Marquess of Lansdowne, William Petty-FitzMaurice. After the Great Famine of the mid-19th century Kenmare became famous for the award-winning lace produced by an industry established by the Poor Clare sisters to alleviate poverty in the town.

Kenmare Bay is famous for its seals – it's home to around 150 harbour seals – and seal-watching cruises run from Kenmare pier. You might also be lucky enough to spot a white-tailed eagle, recently reintroduced to Ireland.

Taking the road west from Kenmare, the first stop is the small village of Sneem, known as 'the knot in the Ring of Kerry'. It's the starting point for a couple of loop walks, the shorter of which, the 10-kilometre Lomanagh Loop, is an easy walk through lovely scenery. The Sneem Storytelling Festival, held in November, hosts storytellers from around the world.

This part of Kerry has a lot of archaeology – a slight detour from the road to Waterville will take you to Staigue Stone Fort, with views from the top over Kenmare Bay. The well-preserved walls of the ring fort stand up to six metres high – they are very thick, and would have provided ample protection for the medieval chieftain who built it. Local folklore has it that the fairies of Staigue Fort were the rivals of the fairies of Cahergal Fort (see page 86), and frequently pitched themselves against each other in games of Gaelic football when the moon was full.

Along this stretch of coast there are some lovely sandy beaches with fine white sand – White Strand, with its small sheltered bays, Glanbeg Strand/O'Carroll's Cove, famous for its turquoise water, and Derrynane Bay, from which Abbey Island is accessible on foot at low tide. The ruins of Ahamore Abbey, a medieval Augustinian church, can be visited there – the graveyard was the burial place of several notable Irish people, including the 18th-century poet, Tomás Rua Ó Súilleabháin, and Mary O'Connell, wife of Daniel O'Connell. Lamb's Head, which forms a natural harbour, can be reached by a short detour off the road to Derrynane Bay.

The 18th-century Derrynane House was the ancestral home of one of Ireland's greatest statesmen, Daniel O'Connell (1775–1847). It was opened to the public in 1967 and visitors can take a tour of the house, where many artefacts of significance in O'Connell's life are on display, including his deathbed, transported from the Italian city of Genoa. The extensive grounds (now Derrynane National Historic Park) are lovely for a peaceful stroll.

Village of Sneem

The River Sneem flows through the village.

One of the most beautiful spots on the Ring of Kerry is Coomakesta Pass, on the road to Waterville. The pass rises to 215 metres and gives panoramic views over Derrynane Bay.

Continuing on the road to Waterville, another slight detour will take you to Loher Stone Fort, a medieval fortified dwelling with great views over *Ballinskelligs Bay.* The wall surrounding the fort has been reconstructed, but the foundations of the interior rooms are original.

Ballinskelligs Beach, a Blue Flag beach just outside Waterville, is popular for swimming and walking. It's dominated by the remains of the 16th-century tower built

Ballinskelligs Bay
The small pier is the departure point for boats to Skellig Michael.

by the great chieftain McCarthy Mór to protect this stretch of coastline from marauding pirates.

Just outside Waterville you'll catch sight of the stone row at Eightercua, four standing stones dating from 1200 BC. Legend has it that Eightercua is the tomb of the wife of the leader of the Milesians, mythical ancestors of the Irish people.

The village of Waterville is a good place to stop for a breather before travelling on to Ballinskelligs. Waterville is a popular holiday spot, and was a favourite destination of Charlie Chaplin.

Charlie Chaplin
A statue in Waterville erected to the memory of the actor and comic.

The Skellig Islands

The two Skellig islands, *Skellig Michael* and *Little Skellig*, lie 10 kilometres off the coast at Portmagee. The larger island, Skellig Michael, is a UNESCO World Heritage Site. Although it is a very inhospitable place, a monastic settlement was established on the island between the eighth and 10th centuries – the beehive-shaped stone huts that are still standing are evidence of the monks' presence there.

They grew their own food and set up a rainwater collection system, as there is no source of fresh water on the island. The strange landscape led to the island being chosen as a location for two *Star Wars* films. Now the only residents are large seabird populations, including the Atlantic puffins for which the island is famous. Little Skellig has the largest gannet colony in the world. While it is possible to take a boat trip around the islands, only a limited number of visitors are allowed on Skellig Michael, and only between May and October.

The next bit of the route follows Ballinskelligs Bay, with its panoramic views, passing Inny Strand, a long sandy beach that is perfect for swimming. You can take a boat to the Skellig Islands from the small Irish-speaking village of Ballinskelligs (one of the last remaining Irish-speaking areas in Kerry), home to Ballinskelligs Priory, established in the 12th century by the monks of Skellig Michael, who found that they could no longer tolerate the difficult conditions on the island.

A quick detour from the road takes you to Bolus Head, flanking St Finian's Bay. There is a well-signposted nine-kilometre loop walk, which allows you to enjoy views of the Skellig islands, their two peaks rising majestically out of the sea. The remains of an early monastic settlement, Kildreelig, are on the south-eastern slope of Bolus Head. A place of pilgrimage until the beginning of the last century, it is a tranquil spot with stunning views over the Atlantic and as far as the Beara Peninsula.

Back on the route and following the curve of St Finian's Bay, with its attractive beach, the Glen, the Skelligs are constant companions. Follow the route over the breathtaking Coomanaspig Pass (rising to 300 metres), taking in the views of Valentia Island and *Dingle Bay*. Just outside Portmagee are the rugged 300-metre high *Kerry Cliffs* – a 10-minute walk will take you the viewing point, the place on the mainland that is closest to the Skellig Islands. The panorama also includes the *Blasket Islands*.

Kerry Cliffs
Waves lash the Kerry Cliffs, one of the most spectacular cliff ranges in County Kerry.

Portmagee is a busy fishing village, named after notorious smuggler Theobald Magee, a former army officer who took advantage of the fractured Kerry coast to ply his illicit trade. You can take a boat to Skellig Michael from Portmagee – if you want to find out a bit more about the island and its monks without venturing out to sea, visit the Skellig Experience Visitor Centre, a prizewinning exhibition centre on Valentia

Portmagee
The town is known as 'the ferry'.

Island. Boat trips around the Skelligs (without landing), can be booked on the day (depending on sea conditions).

Valentia Island, one of Ireland's most westerly points, is a populated island linked to Portmagee by the Maurice O'Neill Memorial Bridge, which spans the Portmagee Channel. The view of Valentia from the mainland gives the impression of a gentle landscape; however, the north side of the island is rugged and wild, with high cliffs looming over the crashing Atlantic waves.

Newfoundland
Landing of the first
Atlantic telegraph
cable at Trinity Bay,
Newfoundland on 4
August 1858.

Crossing the Atlantic

The first transatlantic telegraph cable was sent from Valentia Island to Newfoundland on 16 August 1858, utilising an undersea cable laid for the purpose. The cable was a congratulatory message from Queen Victoria to President James Buchanan. Although the underwater cable was accidentally destroyed three weeks later, it represented a breakthrough in modern communications.

Valentia is home to one of the great lighthouses of Ireland, located at Cromwell Point in the north-east of the island. It came into operation in 1841 and is still a working lighthouse. It has been automated since 1847. Cromwell Point Lighthouse is open to the public, depending on weather conditions.

Geokaun Mountain in the east of the island is 180 metres high, with four viewing points en route to the summit. At each viewing point there are boards displaying information about the island. The views from the top will reward your efforts – the Skelligs, the Dingle Peninsula, the Blaskets, Portmagee, Cahersiveeen and the MacGillicuddy's Reeks, the highest mountain range in Ireland.

Don't miss the Tetrapod Trackway, the oldest record of a four-legged vertebrate walking on land. It dates from 350 million years ago, when Ireland was part of a large

Cromwell Point Lighthouse
In operation since 1841.

land mass. The creature would have been walking on silt – when the silt turned to stone it captured the ancient footprints that can be seen today.

Glanleam Gardens (Glanleam House was built as a linen mill by the Knight of Kerry in 1775, and now provides private accommodation), a 50-acre lush sub-tropical garden, was laid out by the 19th knight, featuring plant species brought from South America.

The Bray Head Loop is an easy five-kilometre walk from the bridge to the west of the island and back again. It takes you to Bray Tower, an unusual lookout built by British forces in 1815 in the style of a medieval Irish tower house.

The annual Valentia Island King Scallop Festival, a three-day event celebrating the mollusc, is held every July. It's a lot of fun, with scallop-related entertainment for all the family, including cooking demonstrations, live music on the streets and, of course, plenty of scallops.

Back on the mainland, indulge yourself with a trip to the Skelligs Chocolate Factory and Café, where you can take a self-guided tour of the factory and enjoy some delicious chocolate treats in the café.

Ballycarbery Castle, a 17th-century structure believed to have been a McCarthy Mór stronghold, can be seen from the road to Cahersiveen. The castle is now a ruin, but it is clear that it was once a substantial building. Unfortunately, as the owner of the land on which it stands has blocked public access, it can be admired only from a distance.

Just a few hundred metres from the castle is Cahergal Stone Fort, believed to have been constructed in the 7th century AD.

Cahergal Stone Fort
Near Cahersiveen, County Kerry.

It has many similarities with Staigue Stone Fort (see page 72), and has the remains of a circular house inside the outer wall. The remains of a larger fort, Leacanbuaile, are a short walk away. This structure dates from around the 10th century, and there are the remains of several domestic buildings inside the outer wall. Both forts were built in locations with wide-ranging views over the surrounding landscape. Coming back to Cahergal, a left turn at the T-junction leads to the lovely Blue Flag beach of White Strand.

The busy market town of Cahersiveen, situated at the foot of Mount Bentee (376 metres) is one of the westernmost towns in Europe. Daniel O'Connell was born just outside the town on 6 August 1775. He is commemorated in the Daniel O'Connell Memorial Church, one of just a handful of Catholic churches worldwide that are dedicated to lay people. Cahersiveeen hosts a Roots Music Festival each year in May.

Daniel O'Connell

Irish political leader and orator in the first half of the 19th century.

The Bentee Loop is a nine-kilometre walk that will take you to the top of Mount Bentee to enjoy the stunning 365° views over the landscape.

Along the road from Cahersiveen to Glenbeigh is Kells Bay, a Blue Flag beach on Dingle Bay. Overlooking it is Kells Bay Gardens, known to locals as the 'Jewel on the Ring'. A 42-acre garden filled with sub-tropical plants, this is a great place for a family outing. It has a dinosaur garden, and the longest rope bridge in Ireland, the Sky Walk.

The small village of Glenbeigh has many associations with Irish folklore – Diarmuid and Gráinne are said to have hidden in a nearby cave, and beautiful *Rossbeigh Beach*, backed by sand dunes, is where Oisín and Niamh galloped into the sea on their way to Tír na nÓg.

The last stop on the Iveragh Peninsula is the town of Killorglin, most famous for its three-day Puck Fair, one of Ireland's oldest festivals, which is held every August. A wild goat – 'Puck' – is enthroned in commemoration of an event during the Cromwellian era when a herd of wild goats stampeded through the town to warn the inhabitants that Cromwell's army was coming.

Rossbeigh Beach
The *Sunbeam* shipwreck on Rossbeigh beach.

The three-day Flavour of Killorglin Festival, held every September, is a celebration not just of the town's great eating places but of the many local food producers.

Although not on the Wild Atlantic Way, the lively town of Killarney and the Killarney National Park (Ireland's oldest national park) will repay the effort of a slight detour away from the coast.

CHAPTER 4 Dingle Peninsula &
The Shannon Estuary

The cliffs at
Dunquin on the
Dingle Peninsula,
with the Blasket
Islands beyond

What to look out for along the way.

Key towns and villages
Dingle
Tralee
Ballybunion
Ballyheigue

Beaches
Inch Strand; Binn Bán; Kinard Strand; Ventry Bay; Coumeenole Bay; Carrignaparka Beach; Smerwick Harbour; Wine Strand; Fermoyle Strand; Fenit Beach; Ballyheigue Bay; Ballybunion

Viewing points
Ceann na Binne; Cruach Mhartháin; Clogher Head; Smerwick Harbour; Dooneen Pier; Bromore Cliffs

Monuments
Minard Castle; Dunbeg Fort; Fahan; Reask Monastery; Gallarus Oratory; Gallarus Castle; Kilmalkedar; Carrigafoyle Castle; Ardfert; Rattoo Monastery and Round Tower; Ballybunion Castle; Lislaughtin Friary

Garden
Garden of the Senses, Tralee

Walks
Dingle Harbour Walk; Siúlóid na Cille; Siúlóid na Faille

Offshore islands
The Blaskets

Food and drink
Dingle Food Festival (October)

Festivals
Kerry Camino Walking Festival (May); Rose of Tralee (August); Féile na Bealtaine, Dingle (May); Festival of Lúnasa, Cloghane (July)

Don't miss!
The Blasket Centre, Dunquin; Brandon Creek; Blennerville Windmill; Tralee Bay Wetlands Centre; Fungi the dolphin, Dingle Bay; Beehive huts, Fahan; The Reask Stone; Dingle Races (August)

Inch Strand

The Dingle Peninsula section of the Wild Atlantic Way is a beach-lovers' paradise. The first stretch of coast en route to Dingle town has plenty to choose from for swimmers, surfers and walkers, from the more than five-kilometre sandy expanse of *Inch Strand* on a spit jutting out into the sea, to Minard Beach, overlooked by the remains of a 16th-century tower house, and Kinard Strand, with its rocky sentinel, An Starrach. Dún Síon, near Kinard,

is a beautiful beach, but has very strong currents and is unsuitable for swimming.

The ruin of Minard Castle, which dominates Kilmurry Bay, was a FitzGerald stronghold built in the second half of the 16th century. Less than a century later it was breached by Cromwellian troops. The inhabitants were slaughtered and the castle was abandoned.

The route moves back to the coast, behind Minard Castle, to pass through the tiny village of Annascaul, built close to the spot where legendary hero Cúchulainn is said to be buried.

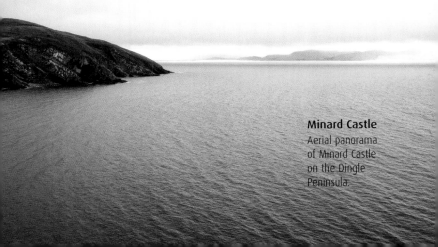

Minard Castle

Aerial panorama of Minard Castle on the Dingle Peninsula.

Fungi

The focal point of the Dingle Peninsula is the lively town of Dingle, Europe's westernmost town. It's located on Dingle Bay, probably most famous for its resident bottlenose dolphin, Fungi, who arrived in 1983. Boat trips are offered around the bay for an almost guaranteed sighting of the friendly mammal.

Dingle is one of those Irish towns where there always seems to be something happening, even in the winter months. With a full calendar of festivals throughout the year, as well as the usual local events, including an international film festival in March, a four-day arts and music festival, Féile na Bealtaine, in early May, the fun-filled Dingle Races in August, and a Food Festival in October. If you feel overwhelmed by the constant activity, chill out on the eight-kilometre Harbour Walk, which takes you out of town eastwards to the lighthouse and the lovely beach at Binn Bán. An easy climb to the top of Ceann na

Slea Head

Binne will allow you to enjoy superb views over Dingle.

Travelling west from Dingle along the winding Slea Head Drive towards *Slea Head* you will arrive at Ventry Bay, a long sheltered beach, good for swimming and snorkelling. If you're feeling energetic, you can hike to the rocky pinnacle of Cruach Mhartháin for great views over this part of the peninsula and out to the Blasket Islands.

Dunbeg Fort
A Bronze Age fort at Slea Head.

The first stop after Ventry, perched almost at the edge of the cliffs of Dingle Bay, is one of Dingle's many ancient monuments. Dunbeg Fort dates from the Bronze Age, and was in use until medieval times. It is a promontory fort, which means that it relied on its position for much of its defences. The coast has been eroded over the centuries, so the well-chosen location of the fort is now putting it in a precarious position where it is in danger of falling into the sea. Close to Dunbeg is Fahan, a substantial cluster of drystone beehive huts, or clochán, similar to those found on Skellig Michael, dating from the eighth century AD.

Slea Head, at the southern tip of the Dingle Peninsula, is very dramatic, with cliffs to one side and the Atlantic on the other, and a wonderful view out to the Blasket Islands. Rounding the corner from Slea Head you'll come across Coumeenole Bay, one of the most dramatic beaches in Ireland. At high tide, the sea swallows up this golden beach, advancing right up to the cliffs.

Blaskets View, on the western tip of the peninsula, has stunning views over Blasket Sound, and a beautiful beach, Carrignaparka.

View from Dunquin
Rain moves in from the west across the Blasket Islands and Blasket Sound.

The Blasket Islands

The largest of the Blasket Islands, Great Blasket, was inhabited until 1953, despite its inhospitable climate. Life on the Irish-speaking island was very simple, with farming, fishing and weaving the main activities. In November 1953 the Irish government evacuated the 22 people living

there on the grounds that life was becoming increasingly unsustainable. The islanders were resettled at Dunquin. At that time there was only one child, so the island population would probably have died out eventually. The island produced a number of storytellers and writers, including Muiris Ó Súilleabháin and Peig Sayers. It is possible to visit this beautiful place (you can overnight in self-catering accommodation or in the island's hostel, which is open during the summer months, travelling on one of a number of boats offering trips to the island, which is now home to a large colony of grey seals.

While you can't stay on the smaller Blasket Islands, you can take a boat trip from Ventry to get a closer look.

Travelling towards the northern side of the peninsula, stop at *Dunquin Pier* for the stunning views. A narrow pathway leads to a departure point for ferries to the Blaskets. The Blasket Centre at Dunquin is an outstanding visitor centre that tells the story of the islands. The centre is the starting point for Siúlóid na Cille, a manageable five-kilometre coastal and hill walk – look out for the schoolhouse built for the filming of the epic romantic drama *Ryan's Daughter* (1970).

Just north of Dunquin is Clogher Head, where you can pull in and enjoy one of the best views along this stretch of the coast, taking in *Mount Brandon*, the Three Sisters (with their curiously masculine names) and Sybil Head. Nearby is Clogher Strand, a nice sandy beach, although its strong currents make it unsuitable for swimming.

The route then cuts off the next promontory on the peninsula, arriving at Smerwick Harbour, a series of small linked beaches ending at Wine Strand. It's a lovely spot for swimming or walking, or just taking in the superb views.

Just behind Wine Strand is the monastic site at Reask, one of many such sites on Slea Head. Reask is notable for its cross slabs, including the beautifully decorated Reask Stone. The site of this monastery was most recently used as a burial ground for unbaptised children.

The Three Sisters
Binn Hanraí, Binn Meanach and Binn Diarmada.

A little north of Wine Strand you can take advantage of the opportunity for a bit of indulgence at Spá Atlantach in Ballydavid, one of several seaweed spas that can be found along the Wild Atlantic Way, using the mineral-rich seaweed that is so abundant along the Atlantic coastline. Immerse yourself in a warm seaweed bath in complete privacy, or have a relaxing massage treatment.

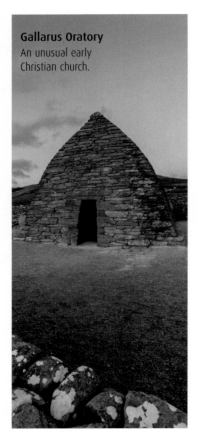

Gallarus Oratory
An unusual early
Christian church.

Overlooking Smerwick Harbour, the almost perfectly preserved medieval Gallarus Oratory is one of the most iconic images of the Dingle Peninsula. Unlike the more usual drystone beehive huts, the oratory is shaped rather like the hull of an upside-down boat. A single small window admits a little light. Legend has it that the soul of anyone who could achieve the impossible task of climbing through the tiny window would be purified. It's a peaceful place if you can visit at a quiet time, but the existence of a visitor centre is evidence of the popularity of the site. The visitor centre is closed in the winter months.

Worth a visit while you're in the area is Gallarus Castle, about a kilometre from the oratory. A restored four-storey FitzGerald tower house dating from the 16th century, this is one of only a few fortified structures on the Dingle Peninsula.

Nearby Kilmalkedar, on an ancient pilgrim route running from Ventry to Mount Brandon, has associations with St Brendan the Navigator and is regarded as one of the most important ecclesiastical sites in the country.

Two of the buildings in the 10-acre complex are St Brendan's House and St Brendan's Oratory (not dissimilar to the oratory at Gallarus in style). On one side of the path leading to the beautiful Romanesque church is an ogham stone, almost two metres high, and on the other, is a standing stone sundial. The church, believed to date from the middle of the 12th century, is one of several stone-roofed churches in Ireland (a small portion of the roof is still intact).

Kilmalkedar Stone
Inscribed in ogham, a Celtic writing system.

Brandon Creek

After Kilmalkedar, follow the road north-west to Dooneen Pier, from where there is a sweeping view over the bay, flanked by the Three Sisters. A little further on is the tiny village of Ballydavid – there is a six-kilometre signposted loop walk, Siúlóid na Faille, from the pier. The first part of the walk goes along the coast, and then loops back through the interior countryside.

Brandon Creek, in the shadow of Mount Brandon, is a little cove from where St Brendan set sail in AD 535 on the voyage during which he is said to have landed on a whale and, later, discovered North America. While it may seem far-fetched, in 1976 the explorer Tim Severin reconstructed the saint's voyage in a boat constructed from materials that would have been available in Brendan's time, making landfall in Newfoundland in June 1977, a little more than a year after setting out.

Doubling back to Dingle town, you can drive towards Fermoyle Strand along one of the most scenic (and one of the highest) roads in Ireland, the Conor Pass. Rising to 450 metres along just over seven kilometres, this road is not for the faint-hearted driver, but if you do make the journey you'll be rewarded at the highest point (where you can park) with incomparable views from the Brandon Mountains.

The longest strand in Ireland (almost 20 kilometres) begins in the area of two small traditional seaside villages, Cloghane and Brandon, and incorporates the beaches of Fermoyle, Kilcummin, Gowlane, Stradbally and Fahamore.

Cloghane is in the Gaeltacht and is therefore an Irish-speaking village, and has a rich heritage of traditional music, storytelling and dancing. In the last weekend in July the Cloghane area hosts the Festival of Lúnasa, a family-oriented event that showcases local artists and includes a blessing of the boats.

Rose of Tralee Festival
Fireworks reflected in water during the festival.

Seven kilometres north of Cloghane is Brandon Point, a popular bird-watching platform, especially in the autumn, when strong winds carry birds into the bay.

The Wild Atlantic Way runs parallel to the coast from *Castlegregory* to Tralee, Kerry's county town and host to the annual international Rose of Tralee Festival. The dominant landmark here is the picturesque Blennerville Windmill, an early 19th-century windmill which now houses a visitor centre and an exhibition of historic artefacts.

A popular Tralee attraction is the Tralee Bay Wetlands

Centre, an 8,000-acre nature reserve which has an activity zone that includes water activities and a climbing wall, a nature zone with guided boat tours and nature trails, and a 20-metre viewing tower with vistas over the reserve to the Slieve Mish Mountains and out into the bay.

The 35-acre Tralee Town Park, in the centre of the town, is a pleasant place for a stroll. The Garden of the Senses is a small sculpture garden within the confines of the park, displaying sculptures on themes of Irish history and mythology that represent the senses.

Close to Tralee is the popular Fenit Beach, with views out into Tralee Bay and Fenit or Little Samphire lighthouse, built in the mid-19th century. You can take a boat trip out to the lighthouse for a guided tour.

St Brendan the Navigator was born in Fenit in AD 484, and a powerful bronze statue of the saint was erected on Samphire Island in 2004.

St Brendan the Navigator
Four-metre high statue on Samphire Island.

The Kerry Camino

Modelled on the famous Camino de Santiago in northern Spain, the Kerry Camino starts in Tralee and ends in Dingle.

You can take a three-day guided walk and have your camino passport (available free of charge at local tourist offices) endorsed at stamping stations along the spectacularly beautiful 57-kilometre route. There is a Kerry Camino Walking Festival in May.

The road northwards from Tralee will take you to the ecclesiastical complex of Ardfert, the oldest portions of which are believed to date from the 11th century. In the 12th century Ardfert became a large diocese, and the size of the cathedral reflects its importance. The building was modified over the centuries, with Romanesque and Gothic elements. There is also smaller church in the complex and a third, attached to Ardfert Friary, just down the road from the cathedral.

Ballyheigue is a popular seaside town with a 10-kilometre stretch of sandy beach, which gets very busy in the summer months. At low tide you can walk out to the tiny island of Black Rock.

Rising out of the sixth-century monastery complex at Rattoo, the 28-metre round tower is considered to be one of the finest in the country. The sandstone tower is unusual in that it is built on a masonry base and was originally accessed by a causeway (this no longer exists). Look out for the sheela-na-gig carved over one of the windows.

With its two stunning sandy beaches, *Ballybunion* is one of Ireland's top seaside destinations. When the Irish weather lets you down you can relax in the century-old

Collins's Hot Seaweed Baths on Ladies' Beach, with the sound of the sea in the background.

The ruin of Ballybunion Castle, one of 15 cliff forts on the North Kerry coast, dominates the sandy beaches of this holiday resort. Built by the FitzMaurices in the 16th century on the site of an earlier promontory fort, it was badly damaged in a raid in 1582. It must have been attacked frequently – a network of escape tunnels was discovered underneath. It has been a national monument since 1923.

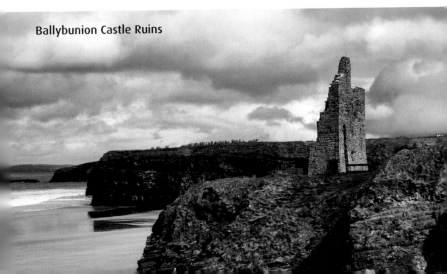

Ballybunion Castle Ruins

Bromore Cliffs
A sea stack at
Bromore Cliffs.

Just a few kilometres north of Ballybunion are the spectacular Bromore cliffs. The soft stone from which they have been formed has been eroded by the sea, creating numerous caves and sea stacks. They are home to a wealth of wildlife of all types. A colony of grey seals has its home in one of the caves, and the last Irish eagles nested in one of the sea stacks. The remains of a promontory fort, believed to date from the Bronze Age, were excavated on the cliffs, and a Second World War lookout post was built on the same promontory, taking advantage of the highly strategic location.

Rounding the northern corner of this stretch of coast and heading eastwards into the Shannon Estuary, you will find *Carrigafoyle Castle*, a five-storey O'Connor stronghold that dominates the southern bank of the estuary. In 1580, during the

Field Marshal Sir William Pelham
Lord Justice of Ireland, by Hieronimo Custodis, after a painting attributed to Cornelis Ketel.

Second Desmond Rebellion, the castle was attacked by crown forces, led by Sir William Pelham. The garrison was massacred and the castle was badly damaged.

Having taken Carrigafoyle, Pelham moved on to the nearby Franciscan friary at Lislaughtin, founded in 1477 by John O'Connor and built in the O'Connor demesne. A major artefact associated with the friary, the Ballymacasey Cross, was unearthed in 1871 by a farmer ploughing his field. It is believed that the monks buried the great processional crucifix for safekeeping before fleeing Pelham's forces with whatever they could carry.

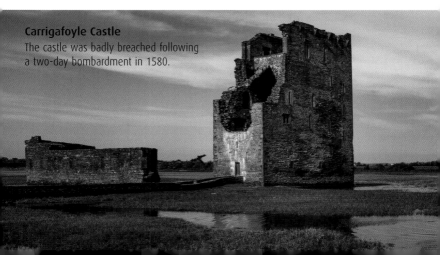

Carrigafoyle Castle
The castle was badly breached following a two-day bombardment in 1580.

CHAPTER 5 The Cliff Coast

Loop Head
Peninsula in West
Clare

CHAPTER 5 Glin to The Burren

What to look out for along the way.

Key towns and villages
Glin
Foynes
Kilrush
Carrigaholt
Kilkee
Doonbeg
Lahinch
Milltown Malbay
Lisdoonvarna
Doolin
Ballyvaughan

Viewing Points
Loop Head; Cliffs of Moher;
Quilty; the Bridges of Ross;
Kilkee Cliffs; Clahane; Hag's
Head; Black Head; Loop Head

Beaches
Kilkee; Doonaha; White Strand
(Doonbeg); Lahinch (good for
surfing); Spanish Point; Fanore;
Bishop's Quarter

Monuments
Glin Castle; Carrigaholt Castle; Corcomroe Monastery; Poulnabrone Dolmen; Tawnagh Mill; O'Brien's Tower; Caherdoonish Stone Fort; Gleninagh Castle; Corcomroe Abbey

Gardens
Boyce's Gardens, Foynes; Doolin Garden; Knockpatrick Gardens, Foynes; Caher Bridge Garden, Fanore; Vandeleur Walled Garden, Kilrush

Walks
Loop Head; Kilkee Cliff Walks; Doolin to Liscannor Coast Walk; Ballyvaughan Wood Loop; Black Head Loop

Food and Drink
Burren Slow Food Festival (May); Carrigaholt Oyster and Trad Music Festival (May); Seafood in September, Carrigaholt; The Burren Winterage Weekend (October)

Offshore Island
Scattery Island

Music
Willie Clancy Week (July); Kilrush Trad Music and Set-Dancing Festival (July/August)

Don't Miss!
The Flaggy Shore
Aillwee Cave
Burren Limestone Coast
Foynes Flying Boat Museum
Burren National Park
Doolin Cave
Dolphin-watching (south of Carrigaholt)
Lisdoonvarna Matchmaking Festival (September)
Doolin Cave

On the county border with Kerry and Limerick is the small town of Glin, centred on the 18th-century town square. Glin Castle is a Georgian mansion built in the late 18th century near the ruins of the original castle, which dates from the early 13th century, and is the ancestral home of the Knights of Glin.

The village of Foynes, situated in the hills at the edge of the Shannon Estuary, is a major sea port and has played an important part in the history of transatlantic aviation. Before airplanes had enough flying range to cross the Atlantic, seaplanes were used for the journey, and Foynes was the last port of call for those travelling to the ocean's western shores. A flying boat terminal was built at Foynes

Foynes 1938
Taking a boat out to a flying boat at Foynes.

in 1935 and it became one of the largest civilian airports in Europe during the Second World War. When Shannon Airport opened in 1942 the days of the Foynes terminal were numbered and it was closed in 1946. In 1988 a portion of the old terminal was opened to the public as a museum. One of the Foynes Flying Boat Museum's exhibits is a full-sized replica of the Boeing 314 flying boat.

The award-winning Knockpatrick Gardens, established as a garden almost a century ago by the current owner's father, is a must-see for gardening enthusiasts. The three-acre site has a wonderful display of flowering plants and mature trees. The garden is open from April until October.

Boeing 314

These flying boats were in service from 1939 to 1948. Passengers on transatlantic flights paid around €10,000 at today's prices, but enjoyed luxury service.

Scattery Island
Home to Ireland's
second-tallest
round tower.

The easiest way to get to the next stage of the Wild Atlantic Way is to double back into Tarbert in County Kerry and take the *Tarbert–Killimer car ferry* to Killimer in County Clare. Crossings are frequent. Call in to Boyce's Gardens at Mountrenchard en route to the ferry for a stroll around this delightful one-acre garden designed for year-round colour.

A few kilometres to the west of Killimer is Kilrush, the main town on the West Clare Peninsula. An Irish Heritage town with a long maritime tradition, it is a good base for exploring the dramatic scenery and beautiful beaches of this part of Clare. If you visit Kilrush at the end of July or the beginning of August you can take part in the Kilrush Traditional Music and Set Dancing Festival.

The two-acre Vandeleur Walled Garden is worth a visit – it was established in woodland in the Vandeleur Demesne in Victorian times, and there is a wonderful period glasshouse, some interesting water features, an unusual horizontal maze and a giant chessboard, and some wonderful planting that takes advantage of the prevailing warm micro-climate.

There are ferries from Kilrush to *Scattery Island*, which has a long association with Christianity and has no fewer than six churches. St Senan founded a monastery there to take advantage of the island's peace and tranquillity, but this haven was invaded many times by Vikings and Danes. The second tallest round tower in Ireland is on Scattery, built to protect the monks from the invading hordes – to no avail; the Vikings decided to settle there, until they were ousted by Brian Boru in 977.

Brian Boru

Carrigaholt, a small fishing village at the mouth of the Moyarta River in *Carrigaholt Bay*, is most famous for its 15th-century castle, family seat of the MacMahons. The castle became forfeit to the crown in the reign of Elizabeth I, and was granted to the MacMahon's traditional enemies, the O'Briens. After the Battle of the Boyne, the Jacobite O'Briens forfeited their lands and properties, which were granted to the Burton family, who lived in the castle until the end of the 19th century.

Carrigaholt Castle
The castle was built c.1480 by the MacMahons.

Bottlenose Dolphin

The green waters off the coast of Carrigaholt are home to the largest school of bottlenose dolphins in Europe.

Carrigaholt is a fish and seafood lovers' mecca. Each May it marries two of its best traditions in the Oyster and Trad Festival. The Seafood in September Festival is held every September. Apart from the usual food festival events, there are opportunities to catch and cook your own fish and demonstrations of fish filleting and seafood preparation. Don't miss the lovely sandy beach at Doonaha.

The River Shannon ends its journey into the Atlantic just south of Carrigaholt. This part of the coast is a designated Special Area of Conservation and is home to the largest group of bottlenose dolphins in Europe. There are boat trips that allow you to enjoy the wildlife and history of the area, with plenty of opportunities for dolphin sightings, although these, of course, can't be guaranteed.

Loop Head, at the tip of the peninsula that bears its name, is a dramatic vantage point, marking the spot where the Shannon enters the Atlantic. In one direction are the calm waters of the Shannon Estuary, while the wild Atlantic waters crash against the rocks on the other side. The four-kilometre walk from the Loop Head lighthouse to the beach at Fodry will allow you to take in the majestic wildness of the place.

On the north-westwards route along the Atlantic side of the peninsula, the *Bridges of Ross* are believed to be one of the best vantage points in Europe from which to watch the sea. On the west of Ross Bay, facing into the Atlantic, they are not visible from the road, but are just a few hundred metres from the Ross Bay car park. Although only one of the natural sea arches remains (two of them collapsed into the sea in the 20th century), the plural name persists.

The Bridges of Ross

Kilkee Cliffs, 3.5 kilometres south of Kilkee town, are as spectacular as the Cliffs of Moher, but are not on the international tourist trail so they don't attract throngs of sightseers. The approach from Kilkee beach is the easiest, and there are a couple of very manageable signposted loop walks.

The town of Kilkee, built around horshoe-shaped Moore Bay, was a popular Victorian watering hole, and is still a busy holiday destination. Protected by the Duggerna Reef, the extensive beach is one of the safest on the west coast, and the nearby Pollock Holes, carved out of the rocks by the sea, are safe swimming

Doonbeg Beach

Popular with holidaymakers escaping the crowds at Kilkee.

and snorkelling places when the tide is out.

Doonbeg is a small village at the mouth of the Cooraclare River, watched over by the ruin of a 15th-century MacMahon tower house, later an O'Brien fortress. Doonbeg is famous for White Strand, a Blue Flag beach four kilometres north of the village.

Don't miss the tiny village of Quilty, which has amazing views out to the Aran Islands and over to the Cliffs of Moher. On a clear day you can even see the Kerry Mountains. It's a bad part of the coast for shipping, and one of the ships of the Spanish

Clare Island
The lighthouse
protects the coast
at Spanish Point.

Armada was wrecked near Lurga Point in 1588. There were
some survivors, who managed to struggle to land, but they
were all captured and hanged by the British. *Spanish Point*,
a little further north, has a lovely beach for swimming and
surfing.

Mutton Island, off Quilty, is believed to have become
separated from the mainland by a tidal wave in the ninth
century. It was inhabited until the 1920s, but is now just a
grazing place for sheep and home to two forts and several
abandoned houses. Although there is no ferry to the island,
which has no landing stage, it is sometimes possible to
walk there at low tide.

Milltown Malbay, near Spanish Point, was, as the name suggests, a milling hub, where local farmers came to have their grain milled in one of five mills. These days, it's better known as an international centre of Irish traditional music, hosting the Willie Clancy Week each July.

The lively little resort of *Lahinch* on Liscannor Bay is something of an international mecca for surfers, while the marshes just north of the town are a birdwatchers' paradise. The best views over Liscannor Bay can be enjoyed at *Clahane*, to the west of Lahinch.

The next stretch of the Wild Atlantic Way takes you over the *Cliffs of Moher*, a stunning formation of cliffs soaring 214 metres out of the sea. The area around the visitor centre and O'Brien's Tower can get very crowded, and one of the best ways to appreciate the cliffs is to take the 18-kilometre Cliff Walk from Liscannor Bay to Doolin, a tiny village that is a gateway to both the Aran Islands and The Burren. This route passes Hag's Head, a headland from which there are outstanding views of the cliffs. Don't miss Doolin Cave, home to the largest stalactite in the northern hemisphere. Doolin Garden, at Ballyvoe, is deceptively simple in its layout, and showcases the plants that grow well in the harsh climate.

Lisdoonvarna, a spa town a little north of Doolin, was very popular in Victorian times. The spa is now closed, but visitors can go to the restored Victorian Pump House and taste the sulphur-rich water. Lisdoonvarna is now more famous for its annual matchmaking festival in September.

Cliffs of Moher
The breathtaking views are among the most popular in Ireland.

The Burren

Although the Burren National Park is not on the route of the Wild Atlantic Way, the detour will take you to one of the strangest landscapes in Europe, an area of such geological significance that in 2015 it was designated a UNESCO Global Geopark, putting it on a par with Newgrange and the Giant's Causeway. The western boundary of the park runs along the coast, and is known as the Burren Limestone Coast, while to the south and east, the limestone slabs gradually merge with green farmland. Although the rocky landscape seems infertile, the fissures between the slabs host an array of unusual plants, including some that are otherwise found only in Alpine regions. There are several signposted trails through the Burren, and guided tours are offered in the summer months.

The Aillwee Cave, in the heart of the Burren, with its entrance on the side of a mountain, is one of the oldest caves in Ireland. A guided tour will take you through beautiful caverns, past strange rock formations and alongside a rushing waterfall. You will even see the bones of animals that are now extinct.

The iconic Poulnabrone Dolmen, the second-largest portal tomb in Ireland, was constructed around 6,000 years ago during the Neolithic period. The three standing stones support a horizontal capstone. When it was excavated in 1985, the remains of 33 people were found. Its inaccessible location suggests that it may have been a territorial marker. It was used for ritual well into the Celtic era. It is now possible to drive to the site of the dolmen, but there is a barrier to prevent tourists coming too close to it.

The three-day Burren Slow Food Festival takes place in Lisdoonvarna every May,

Poulnabrone Dolmen

Neolithic portal tomb.

showcasing the best elements of food culture in County Clare. The Burren Winterage Weekend, hosted in October each year, has a wider focus, celebrating the Burren's farming heritage. With food, music and family events, the weekend finishes with a community cattle drive into the hills of the Burren where the animals will spend the winter.

Pamper yourself with a stop at the Burren Perfumery in Carron, a small-batch perfumery where you can take a guided tour in the afternoons from April to September, getting a behind-the-scenes look at how the perfumes and skincare products are made. The Hazel Mountain Chocolate Factory at Oughtmama also offers tours.

Fanore, halfway up the coast, is the main beach on this part of the coastline. At the furthest point north, before the coast heads eastwards towards Galway, is Black Head, with its lighthouse, another excellent viewing point. Enthusiastic walkers might like to walk the Black Head loop, a 26-kilometre hike that takes you right into the Burren. Caherdoonish stone fort, built high on a ridge at Black Head, dates from the early medieval period. Although the views are stunning, it is a desolate spot, and the fabled home to a banshee.

From Black Head in the direction of Galway, an unfrequented track leading to the water's edge will take you to Gleninagh Castle, a 15th-century tower house built by the Princes of the Burren, the O'Loughlins. A holy well, still a site of pilgrimage, was the castle's water source.

On the road to Galway, *Ballyvaughan* is the starting point of an eight-kilometre loop walk. It also has a good beach, known as Bishop's Quarter, just to the north of the village.

The Flaggy Shore, immortalised in Seamus Heaney's poem 'Postscript' (1996), stretches from the beach at New Quay to Finvarra Point, easily identified by its Martello tower. It's an easy walk on a paved road, taking you through an area of such great geological importance that it is a designated site of geological importance within the Burren UNESCO Global Geopark. It's a peaceful place for a walk with wonderful ocean views – you will walk along limestone pavements, encountering fossils and stones that provide clues about the geological history of the area.

In a green valley lying against the backdrop of the Burren is the monastic foundation of Corcomroe, a Cistercian abbey founded in the last years of the 12th century by Donal Mór O'Brien, King of Thomond. The early 13th-century church has some wonderfully elaborate carvings. Legend has it that when the work was finished the king had the masons killed so that they couldn't replicate their carvings elsewhere.

At first sight, Tawnagh Mill, on the road to Traught, appears to be yet another of the many fortified structures that dot this part of the west coast. However, it is actually a tidal mill, one of several built in the early 19th century. It operated at high tide only, when the force of the water turned the grinding mechanism.

Ballyvaughan Bay

CHAPTER 6 The Connemara Coast

Galway Bay at sunset

What to look out for along the way.

Key towns and villages
Galway
Kinvara
Spiddal
Roundstone
Clifden
Carraroe
Cleggan

Viewing Points
Dermot's Bed; Renvyle Point; Dún Aonghasa; Diamond Hill; Synge's Chair

Beaches
Traught; Silverstrand; Spiddal; An Trá Mór; Coral Beach; Gorteen; Dog's Bay; Aillebrack; Salthill; Coral Strand; Bunowen; Glassilaun

Monuments

Dunguaire Castle; Patrick Pearse's Cottage; Dún Aonghasa; Dún Eoghanachta; Cill Einne; Clifden Castle; Renvyle Castle; Knockbrack Tomb; Dún Chonchúir; Kylemore Abbey House and Gardens; Errislannan Manor Gardens, Clifden

Walks

Salthill Promenade; Carraroe Walk; Inishnee Walk; Omey Island Walk; Famine Walk (Killary); Derrigimlagh Loops; Upper Diamond Walk, Letterfrack

Food and Drink

The Galway International Oyster and Seafood Festival (September); Bia Bó Finne (October)

Offshore Island

Aran Islands; Inch; Inishbofin; Macdara's Island

Festivals

Galway International Arts Festival (July); Connemara Pony Show (August); Féile an Dóilín, Carraroe (August); Clifden Arts Festival (September)

Don't Miss!

Lettermore Causeway
The Sky Road
Omey Island (tidal)
Rosroe Pier
Derrigimlagh
Killary Harbour (Ireland's only fjord)
Poll na bPéist
J.M. Synge's House
The Plassey
Cnoc Suain
Roundstone Bog
Ceardlann Spiddal Craft Village
Omey Horse Races (August)

The pretty seaside village of Kinvara is just over the county border between Clare and Galway. The Blue Flag beach at *Traught*, a little north of the village, is popular with holidaymakers. At the far end of the village, picturesque Dunguaire Castle is a draw for summer visitors. This O'Hyne stronghold was built in the 16th century in a strategic position, surrounded by the waters of Galway Bay on three sides and connected to the mainland by a single narrow causeway. It was partially restored by the writer Oliver St John Gogarty, who bought it in 1929. He hosted literary gatherings of the Celtic Revival there – guests included such luminaries as W.B. Yeats. The castle is open to the public and hosts medieval banquets in the summer.

TRAUGHT BEACH

Oyster Contest
Contestants compete in the World Oyster Opening Championship on the second day of the Galway International Oyster and Seafood Festival, 2019.

On the other side of Galway Bay, the busy, colourful city of Galway is a good starting point for the Connemara coast section of the Wild Atlantic Way. If you visit between May and October don't miss Trad on the Prom, which coincides in September with the Galway International Oyster and Seafood Festival, the world's longest-running oyster festival (the first one was held in 1954). The city also hosts the Galway International Arts Festival every July.

Within the city limits Salthill is a busy place with a Blue Flag beach and a good swimming place at Blackrock Baths. Just two kilometres outside the city is *Silverstrand*, a sandy beach that is very popular with locals and visitors. The long *promenade* is a popular place for a bracing walk.

Leaving the city you'll come to Spiddal, a village in the Connemara Gaeltacht, and a base for schoolchildren perfecting their Irish language skills. It can get crowded in the summer. Ceardlann Spiddal Craft Village produces a wide range of hand-crafted products and welcomes visitors who want to observe the craftworkers in action.

While the wide sandy beach at *Spiddal* is very popular, An Trá Mhór (which translates as the Big Strand), a Blue Flag beach three kilometres west of the town at Inverin, is excellent for swimming and has great views along the coast.

Cnoc Suain is an award-winning cultural centre in Moycullen, where visitors can immerse themselves in the nature and heritage of the region, staying in authentically restored cottages.

Aer Arann flies from just outside Inverin to all three Aran Islands (*Inishmore*, *Inishmaan* and *Inisheer*), and the busy fishing port of Rossaveel, a little further along the coast, is the ferry departure point for the three islands.

Beach at Spiddal

The shallow waters of the wide sandy beach are
sheltered by a pier.

The Aran Islands

The Aran Islands have been inhabited since the Bronze Age at least. Rugged, largely devoid of vegetation and exposed to the Atlantic, they seem to be a world apart, although transport links are good. Inishmore is the largest of the three islands and the most visited. The best way to get around is by bike, taking the 26-kilometre (mostly flat) loop around the island. If you prefer to travel on foot, there are three signposted walks, all beginning and ending in Kilronan.

The scenic cliffs of Inishmore, Aran Islands.

Dún Aonghasa

The must-see on Inishmore is Dún Aonghasa, the huge
Bronze Age fort perched at the edge of a cliff on the wild,
south-western side of the island. It is thought that the fort
was built for ceremonial or religious purposes. The original
structures were enclosed within massive drystone walls
during the medieval period, when the Aran Islands were
a disputed territory – their strategic position meant that
whoever controlled them controlled Galway Bay and its
shipping routes. It is now a National Monument.

At the foot of the cliffs just to the east of Dún Aonghasa,
is the remarkable Poll na bPéist (the Wormhole), a perfect
rectangle cut from the rocks by the sea. The waves are
unpredictable, so take care if you decide to have a look.

Dún Aonghasa is not the only stone fort on the island, although it is the most impressive. Dún Eoghanachta, Dún Eochla and Dún Dúcathair (the Black Fort) are all worth visiting.

St Enda's monastic foundation at Killeany (Cill Éinne) was of great importance in the early Irish Church, and many of the luminaries in the pantheon of early Irish saints studied there, including Brendan of Clonfert and Ciarán of Clonmacnoise.

Wave Power Poll na bPéist, cut into the rock by the power of the Atlantic.

Synge
J. M. Synge on Inishmaan.

Inishmaan, with just one shop and one pub, is the quietest of the three islands, but you'll find a few gems. There are three signposted walks from the pier that will take you past most points of interest.

The playwright J. M. Synge was inspired in his writing by the four summers he spent on the island. The thatched cottage where he stayed has been restored as a museum, Teach Synge, open in the summer. Synge's favourite spot on the island was a low stone wall on the west coast cliffs – it is known as Synge's Chair, and has great views.

Near Teach Synge is Dún Chonchúir, an impressive oval ring fort built in the first century AD on one of the island's highest points.

The little Church of Mary Immaculate was built in 1939 using stones from the ruins of a much older church on the site. It's worth a visit for the lovely Harry Clarke stained-glass windows.

The smallest Aran Island, Inisheer, is a short ferry ride from Doolin, in County Clare. You can rent a bike at the pier, or walk the 10-kilometre circuit of the island. Just beside the pier is a stunning beach, known simply as An Trá (The Strand).

A cargo boat, the M.V. *Plassey*, ran aground off the island's coast in 1960. The entire crew was rescued by the locals using a breeches buoy. The boat was later brought to shore and pulled above the high tide mark. The iconic rusted wreck has remained there ever since.

There are the ruins of two 10th-century churches on the island, dedicated to St Kevin and St Gobnait. O'Brien's Castle (not to be confused with the structure of the same name on the Cliffs of Moher) is a 14th-century tower house, seized from the O'Briens by the O'Flahertys in the 16th century. It was surrendered in 1652, when Cromwell's army occupied the Aran Islands.

M.V. *Plassey*
The rusting hulk of the vessel, originally a WW2 minesweeper.

The small village of Carraroe is famous for the traditional red-sailed fishing boats known as the Galway Hookers. Carraroe hosts a regatta, Féile an Dóilín, on the first weekend in August, showcasing the Hookers and other unique Irish boats, such as currachs. A very manageable eight-kilometre loop, the Carraroe Walk, will take you to the Blue Flag beach Trá an Dóilín (Coral Beach), which is relatively quiet and very good for swimming and snorkelling.

Although the five islands of Ceantar na nOileán are not on the route of the Wild Atlantic Way, they are quiet and peaceful and have some lovely beaches. The small country roads are ideal for walking or cycling. The islands of this

Galway Hooker
One of the traditional wooden boats with red sails competing in a regatta.

small archipelago are linked by bridges or causeways, such as the ***Lettermore Causeway***.

The route along the rugged coast of mid-Connemara will take you to the tiny village of Carna. Every year on 16 July, hundreds of local people take their boats to St Macdara's island to attend a mass in the tiny stone oratory in honour of St Macdara, patron saint of fishermen and sailors. The beautiful little oratory, which had lost its roof over the centuries, was restored in 1975.

If the scenery along the road to the pretty village of Carraroe seems familiar, it may be because this part of Connemara was a favourite subject of Belfast-born artist Paul Henry (1877–1958). He specialised in painting the small cottages, smouldering mountains and cloud-topped hills that are so characteristic of this region.

Pearse's Cottage is a small cottage at Rosmuc, surrounded by some of the most beautiful scenery in the west of Ireland. It was owned by Pádraig Pearse, one of the leaders of the 1916 Rising, and he used to hold summer schools there for the pupils at his Dublin school, St Enda's. It was burned down during the War of Independence, but was later restored, and 100 years after the rising, Pearse's role in the foundation of the state was commemorated by the launch of an interactive visitor centre at the cottage.

Continuing along the jagged coastline you will arrive at the picturesque fishing village of Roundstone. As well as offering great views across the bay, Roundstone has two lovely beaches within walking distance, the beautiful white horseshoe-shaped Dog's Bay and neighbouring Gurteen, which is almost a mirror image. Both beaches are very safe for swimming and are popular in the summer months.

The tiny inhabited island of Inishnee is connected to

Roundstone
Houses and boats in the small harbour.

the mainland by a bridge and there is a good waymarked loop walk.

The route to Clifden runs through a stretch of blanket bog and lakes against the backdrop of the Twelve Bens, the strange landscape teeming with flora and fauna. The walk through the bog from Roundstone to Ballyconneely is recommended for experienced hikers only.

The Ballyconneely Peninsula has a stunning wildflower show during the summer months. It also has some lovely beaches, including Aillebrack and *Bunowen*, and *Coral Strand* at Mannin Bay. Coral Strand is particularly good for snorkelling, with some interesting marine life.

From April to October, Errislannan Gardens, just over six kilometres south of Clifden, has a wonderful display of plants and flowers that are well adapted to the climate and soil in the area.

Derrigimlagh, in the bog south of Clifden, earned its place in history on 15 June 1919, when two British aviators, John Alcock and Arthur Whitten Brown, crash-landed their twin-engined Vickers Vimy aircraft there after a 16-hour flight that had started in Newfoundland, Canada. The crash site was close to another notable location – the Marconi Wireless Telegraph Station, from where the first wireless transatlantic message was sent to Novia Scotia in Canada, in 1907. There's an interesting interactive

Crash landing

Alcock and Brown's Vickers Vimy bomber crash-landed in a bog after flying from St John's, Newfoundland.

five-kilometre loop walk around both sites. The Alcock and Brown landing site has a white cone-shaped concrete marker, and there is a memorial near Clifden.

In a snug position between the Twelve Bens and the Atlantic, the picturesque town of Clifden is known unofficially as 'the capital of Connemara', attracting thousands of visitors each year. Every September it hosts the longest-running community arts festival in Ireland, with a packed programme of music, theatre and literary events. The annual Connemara Pony Show is held in August, with equestrian events, a traditional street market, and displays of arts and crafts and Irish dancing.

Clifden Castle
A Gothic Revival edifice near Clifden.

The Connemara Pony

This stocky little pony is unique to the Connemara region. Measuring no more than 1.5 metres in height, the pony is well adapted to the difficult terrain of the area. The pony's ancestors arrived with the Vikings in the eighth century, but by the 16th century they were running wild in the mountains. Horses that escaped from the wrecks of the

A Connemara pony grazing in the Twelve Bens region.

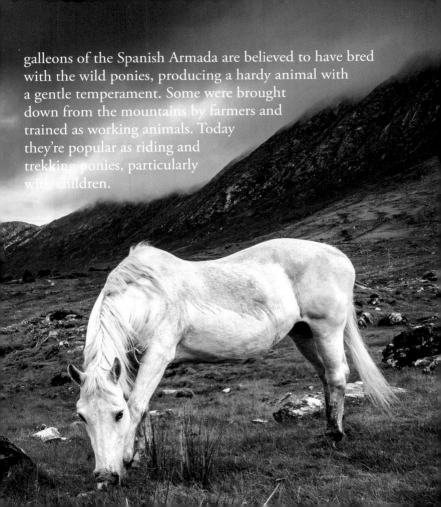

galleons of the Spanish Armada are believed to have bred with the wild ponies, producing a hardy animal with a gentle temperament. Some were brought down from the mountains by farmers and trained as working animals. Today they're popular as riding and trekking ponies, particularly with children.

The Gothic Revival Clifden Castle was built in an elevated position above Clifden in the early 19th century. The owner was John D'Arcy, founder of the town of Clifden. He had a road built from Clifden to Galway, ensuring that this hitherto unknown and impoverished area on the edge of Connemara developed and prospered. D'Arcy's heir failed to live up to his father's ambitions, and when he was declared bankrupt after the hard years of the Great Famine in the mid-19th century, the castle was sold. The castle and its estate were taken over by the state in the early 1920s and the land was distributed to the tenants. The castle fell into ruin and has never been restored.

The 16-kilometre *Sky Road*, beginning and ending in Clifden, is one of the most beautiful routes along the Wild Atlantic Way. It takes you out along the Kingstown Peninsula, with breathtaking views over the sea, the offshore islands, the coastlines of County Mayo to the north and County Clare to the south. The views inland, over the Connemara countryside, are equally stunning.

The Aughrus Peninsula is quiet and sparsely populated, with numerous sandy beaches. Twice a day, at low tide, you can walk, drive or cycle across the beautiful sands at

Omey Island

Dog's Bay to *Omey Island*, a peaceful place renowned for its summer wildflower display. A short 5.5-kilometre loop walk will take you from the car park on the mainland around the island, to enjoy wonderful views of the sea and Friar, High and Cruach Islands. The Omey Horse Races, held at the beginning of August every year, are run on the sands of Dog's Bay.

On the other side of the peninsula is the small fishing village of Cleggan, which came to international attention in 1927 when a terrible fishing disaster claimed 25 lives. The event has been memorialised in poetry and song. *Cleggan Harbour* is the departure point for ferries to *Inishbofin*.

Inishbofin, eight kilometres off the coast, has been inhabited for six millennia and is a haven for many species of wildlife. St Colman of Lindisfarne founded a monastery on the island in the seventh century, having had differences with Rome over the calculation of the date of Easter. Nothing remains of the monastery, but a church was built on the site in the 14th century, and the ruins of this are still standing. With beautiful beaches and quiet walks, it's a good place to spend a night or two. The island hosts a lively arts festival each May, and the very popular Set Dancing and Trad Weekend every autumn. The food festival Bia Bó Finne, held each October, is a celebration of the wonderful organic food produced on the island.

At Knockbrack, just 1.5 kilometres west of Cleggan, there is an outstanding megalithic tomb known as Dermot's (Diarmuid's) Bed. In Irish legend, Diarmuid and Gráinne are said to have sheltered in the tomb while on

Lower Diamond Hill

the run from Fionn Mac Cumhaill. The tomb has a lovely position overlooking Salerna Bay.

The little village of Letterfrack, at the gateway to the Connemara National Park, is famous for its live traditional Irish music. Bog Week and Sea Week, in summer and autumn respectively, bring together musicians and music lovers, for music, discussion and walking sessions. For stunning views, the Upper Diamond Walk from the visitor centre in the park will take you to the top of Diamond Hill.

Kylemore Abbey is a little off the route of the Wild Atlantic Way, but the fairytale setting of the building and the wonderful walled Victorian gardens will reward a detour. The castle was built as a private residence in 1868, but was a Benedictine convent and school from 1920 until 2014.

Connemara's most north-western place, Renvyle Point, at the tip of the Renvyle

Peninsula, has panoramic sea views – on a clear day you can see as far as Croagh Patrick in County Mayo. Medieval Renvyle Castle, now a dangerous ruin, was once the home of the pirate queen, Grace O'Malley, and her husband, Donal O'Flaherty. After O'Flaherty's death, Grace O'Malley returned to the clan territory in County Mayo. Renvyle Castle has a horrible past – the castle was originally a Joyce stronghold, but the O'Malleys are said to have taken possession after murdering all but one of the guests at a wedding there.

Grace O'Malley

Renvyle Castle

Just south of the mouth of Killary Harbour is one of the most beautiful beaches in Ireland – horseshoe-shaped Glassilaun, ideal for snorkelling and swimming in the more sheltered parts.

Killary Harbour forms a dramatic natural border between County Galway and County Mayo and is regarded as Ireland's only fjord. The 15-kilometre Famine Walk starts at picturesque Rosroe Pier and follows the southern side of the harbour as far as Leenane. The track is a 'famine road', built as a famine relief project during the Great Famine. A session at the Connemara Seaweed Baths would be a well-earned treat after your walk.

Glassilaun beach

Aasleagh Falls

What to look out for along the way.

Key towns and villages
Louisburgh
Westport
Killala
Ballycastle
Ballina

Viewing Points
Corraun Peninsula; Doolough Famine Memorial; The Tale of the Tongs; Atlantic Drive; Achill Head; Minaun Heights; Moyteague Head; Doohoma Head; Doonamo Point; Erris Head; Benwee Head; Downpatrick Head

Beaches
Carrowniskey (surfing); Cross Strand; White Strand; Silver Strand; Bertra Strand; Mulranny Beach; Keel Beach; Keem Strand; Elly Bay; Mullaghroe; Termon Beach; Fallmore; Scotch Port; Old Head; Srah

Monuments

Murrisk Abbey; The Boheh Stone; Rockfleet Castle; Castle Kildavnet; East Keel Court Tomb; Knocknaveen; Blacksod Lighthouse; Céide Fields; Moyne Friary; Rosserk Friary; Doonfeeny Standing Stone; Killala Round Tower; Westport House; Dolmen of the four Maols

Walks

Lough Coolaknick Loop; Fawnglass Loop; Knocknaveen Loop; Murrisk Walks; Keem Strand Loop; Newport Village walks; Great Western Greenway (three stages); Children of Lir Loop; Erris Head Loop

Offshore Islands

Inishturk; Clare Island; Achill; Inishbiggle; Claggan; Inishkea

Music

Féile Chois Cuain, Louisburgh (May); The Acoustic Yard Music Festival, Westport (May); Westival, Westport (October)

Don't Miss!

Mweelrea
Aasleagh Falls
National Famine Memorial
Croagh Patrick
Downpatrick Head
Ceathrú Thaidhg
North Mayo Sculpture Trails
Achill Secret Garden
Clew Bay Heritage Centre
SS *Crete Boom*
Ballycroy National Park

The next stage of the route starts at the *Aasleagh Falls* on the River Erriff at the head of *Killary Harbour*. Although Aasleagh is a small waterfall, the setting is beautiful and it's a lovely spot for a picnic. The route goes along the north shore of Killary Harbour and then veers away slightly from the coast, with the highest mountain in Connacht, Mweelrea, looming to the west. The mountain commands great views over the Atlantic and the neighbouring mountains, but it is recommended only for experienced hikers.

Beautiful *Doolough Valley* is the location of a poignant famine memorial, commemorating a group of starving people who trekked from Louisburgh to Delphi Lodge on a freezing day in March 1849 to apply for famine relief. They arrived late and were refused the help they so badly needed. Many died of a combination of hunger, exhaustion and hypothermia on the return journey.

Carrowniskey Strand is a long sandy beach that is popular with swimmers and surfers and can get quite crowded in the summer months. If you double back in a southerly direction, you will find three more good beaches, Cross Strand, White Strand and *Silver Strand*, the last of which is a lovely place for a peaceful and undemanding walk.

You can see *Inishturk Island* from all four beaches, but you'll have to drive north again to get a ferry from *Roonagh Quay* to this tiny peaceful island. There are two signposted loop walks, the shortest of which, the Lough Coolaknick Loop, is only five kilometres long.

Doolough famine memorial

Doolough valley
Looking into the valley along the Bundorragha River.

The Tale of the Tongs

This unusual installation, located above the cliffs on the northern shore of Inishturk, was built to commemorate all those who have emigrated from the island.

It is based on the custom whereby a person would use a tongs to take up a piece of coal and give it to a loved one who was about to emigrate. The coal was then placed in the fire, symbolising a promise by the emigrant to return to the island. *The Tale of the Tongs* is one of the installations on the North Mayo Sculpture Trails (see page 192).

The installation was built in nine days in 2013, using stainless steel, glass and local stone.

The same ferry companies will also take you to the much larger *Clare Island*, whose history is forever linked with that of the O'Malleys, lords of the territory around Clew Bay. The 16th-century tower house at the harbour, one of Grace O'Malley's strongholds, was converted to a police barracks in the 19th century. The very beautiful Cistercian church of St Brigid, dating from the 15th century, has a carved plaque with the O'Malley coat of arms. Next to it is a tomb, said to be Grace O'Malley's.

Grace O'Malley's Tomb

Detail of the altar tomb of Grace O'Malley, pirate queen, in St Brigid's Church.

There is a ruined Napoleonic signal tower at the western end of the island, part of a network built around Ireland at the beginning of the 19th century, when the fear of a French invasion was high.

Quite apart from its more recent historic treasures, Clare Island has many archaeological sites, a couple of good beaches and some world-renowned flora and fauna. There are a couple of easy signposted loop walks, three-kilometre Fawnglass and eight-kilometre Knocknaveen.

Clare Island Country lane leading to the harbour.

Louisburgh is a small town on Clew Bay, home to the Granuaile [Grace O'Malley] Interpretive Centre. You'll find three signposted bike routes through the surrounding countryside, ranging from seven to 26 kilometres in length. Every May the town hosts Féile Chois Cuain, a festival of traditional music, song and dance.

Along the route from Louisburgh to Murrisk there are two lovely beaches, Old Head, which overlooks Croagh Patrick, and Bertra Strand, at the mountain's foot.

Croagh Patrick, or 'the Reek', is Ireland's 'holy mountain', with a long tradition of pilgrimage that predates Christianity. It is believed that in AD 441 St Patrick fasted on top of the mountain for 40 days. On Reek Sunday each July, more than 25,000 pilgrims, some barefoot, climb to

Croagh Patrick
Ireland's Holy
mountain.

the summit. There is a magnificent view of Clew Bay and its 365 islands from the top of the mountain. If you're not equal to the climb, there are four short signposted loop walks from Murrisk car park.

A beautiful site nine kilometres to the west of the town of Westport is home to the National Famine Memorial. Overlooking Clew Bay, John Behan's moving bronze sculpture depicts a 'coffin ship', one of the infamous vessels that brought emigrants to the United States. Instead of sails, skeletons fly from the rigging.

National Famine Memorial
Croagh Patrick is behind the ship, shrouded in mist.

Skeletons
The rigging is a stark reminder of the death toll on the coffin ships.

The Boheh Stone

The Boheh Stone is worth the very short detour from the route. About five kilometres south of Westport, it is one of Ireland's finest examples of Neolithic rock art, with a total of 250 engravings. It is believed to have been a site of ritual celebration – on 18 April and 24 August each year,

Westport Bay and islands with farms and beaches, seen from Croagh Patrick.

the setting sun, when viewed from the stone, rather than sinking behind the summit of Croagh Patrick, appears to roll down the north-western shoulder of the mountain. It somehow became part of the Croagh Patrick Christian pilgrimage and was dubbed 'St Patrick's Chair'.

Murrisk Abbey
The original starting point of the annual Croagh Patrick pilgrimage.

Murrisk Abbey, beneath Croagh Patrick on the shores of Clew Bay, was founded in 1457 as an Augustinian friary. Dedicated to St Patrick, it was the starting point of the Croagh Patrick pilgrimage. The abbey was suppressed by Henry VIII in the early 16th century, but managed to keep going until the 18th century. All that remains of the abbey buildings are a small church and the chapter house, both now roofless.

The lovely town of Westport has a sheltered position in Westport Harbour in the south-eastern corner of Clew Bay. Commissioned in the late 18th century by John Browne,

Westport House
The estate, situated a little outside the centre of the town, has beautiful garden walks.

first Marquess of Sligo, and built by James Wyatt, the town is centred on a graceful Georgian octagonal square. The Brownes, who are direct descendants of Grace O'Malley, own Westport House, an elegant mansion dating from 1730. The house is open to the public, as are the gardens, which incorporate an adventure park.

The Acoustic Yard Festival each May provides an opportunity for singers and songwriters to showcase their work in various small venues around the town, and in October, Westport hosts Westival, a lively music and arts week.

To get an idea of the history of the town and the surrounding area, visit the Clew Bay Heritage Centre on the quays. The centre also offers guided walking tours of the town.

The Wild Atlantic Way hugs the shores of Clew Bay as it travels northwards, passing through the village of Newport, which is a good point from which to explore the countryside on foot or bicycle. There are four signposted loops, ranging in length from six to 12 kilometres.

This part of Mayo was O'Malley territory; the clan built several fortified houses along the coast, the most famous of which is Rockfleet Castle, otherwise known as Carrigahowley Castle, just west of Newport.

The Blue Flag beach at Mulranny is just outside the village at the edge of the Corraun Peninsula. With its long stretch of sand at the edge of clear blue water, it's

Rockfleet Castle

Grace O'Malley stronghold.

popular in the summer months. It's what is known as a storm beach, with large rounded stones and rocks cast up on the shore by the force of the waves during storms. The material is pushed so far up the beach it cannot then be pulled back into the sea by the normal action of the waves.

Mulranny Beach

The Great Western Greenway

This signposted off-road cycling and walking route, opened in 2011, follows the route of the old Westport to Achill railway, covering 42 kilometres in three stages. It's a very scenic route and the absence of traffic means that it is popular with families. Bike hire and accommodation are available along the route.

The route follows the Corraun Peninsula to Ireland's largest island, Achill. It's connected to the mainland by a bridge, so it can feel more like a peninsula than an island. The scenic route around the island is known as the Atlantic Drive and boasts some amazing vistas over the landscape and out to sea and Clare Island. The last stretch ends at Minaun Heights and has the best views on the island.

Sheep on the
Great Western
Greenway trail.

Achill is a beautiful place, with five Blue Flag beaches, the best known of which are *Keel Beach* and *Keem Strand*. Keem is at the end of the road that crosses the island and is very sheltered. Keel is quite exposed to the elements, and is therefore good for surfing and windsurfing. There are three cycling loops around the island and a range of walking opportunities – anything from a gentle stroll to a vigorous hike in the mountains. A seven-kilometre loop begins and ends at Keem Strand, taking you to Achill Head, the westernmost point of the island and a great viewing spot. A vantage point closer to Keem is Moyteague Head, which has the remains of an old watchtower.

Achill Secret Garden, which extends over three acres, takes advantage of the shelter provided by Monterey Cypresses planted about a century ago. It is divided into eight distinct 'chambers' or zones, and guided tours are offered from May to August, when the garden is at its best.

Castle Kildavnet, another O'Malley tower house with particular associations with Grace O'Malley, stands sentinel over Achill Sound. The remains of the medieval church of Kildavnet and its holy well and graveyard are nearby. A steep signposted path from the village of Keel will

Castle Kildavnet at Achill Sound

take you to the East Keel Court Tomb, a Neolithic tomb constructed 5,000 years ago on a beautiful elevated site.

Inishbiggle is a tiny inhabited island off the east coast of Achill in Blacksod Bay. Because of strong currents it can be difficult to get there. You can take a motorised currach from *Doran's Point* on the mainland, or from Bull's Mouth on Achill, sea conditions permitting.

Back on the mainland, the Wild Atlantic Way route goes through Ballycroy National Park, which encompasses the

Owenduff blanket bog and the Nephin Beg mountain range. There is an excellent visitor centre, with an exhibition of the flora, fauna and habitats that can be found in the park, and a two-kilometre nature trail gives views to Achill and the mountains.

Doohooma Head, at the far end of a small peninsula, is a stunningly beautiful long sandy beach, both remote and sheltered, with great views. Further north along the road to Erris Head is tiny *Claggan Island*, connected to the mainland by Srah Green Flag Beach.

The Mullet Peninsula is joined to the mainland by a thin strip of land across Blacksod Bay. The Gaeltacht town of

Ballycroy National Park

Achill Island from the National Park.

Belmullet is at the point where the land connects to the peninsula. It has an unusual 20-metre tidal swimming pool, and two signposted looped cycle routes.

Heading south down the Mullet Peninsula you will find a chain of beaches: *Elly Bay* and Mullaghroe (both Blue Flag), Termon, Fallmore and Cross. The Inishkea Islands can be seen to the west. Blacksod Lighthouse, a substantial granite building at the southern end of the peninsula, lies at the entrance to *Blacksod Bay*. During the Second World War the lighthouse keeper's daily weather reports were phoned to London. On the day scheduled for the D-Day Normandy landings in 1944, he sent a warning of a Force 6 wind, which delayed the landings by one day and probably made all the difference between the success and failure of the mission.

Retracing the route northwards up the peninsula will take you to the ruins of Cross Abbey and a couple of short signposted loop walks, offering a view to the *Inishkea Islands* and Inishglora, the legendary final resting place of the mythical Children of Lir. A little further north is *Doonamo Point*, where you can enjoy the best views on Erris. *Erris Head* is a wild and windy place that feels

Bunwee Head
Wave action in a winter storm.

very remote. At the northern end of the five-kilometre
signposted loop walk around the head there is a railed
viewing point with spectacular views.

Benwee Head is the highest point on the Dún Chaocháin
cliffs. The 12-kilometre loop walk is often referred to
as 'the Children of Lir Loop' – there is a large tubular
installation commemorating the mythical foursome, whose
legend strikes a chord in most Irish hearts.

Continuing along the coast you will soon come to the *Céide Fields*, a Neolithic network of large enclosed fields extending over several thousand acres. The fields were discovered in the 1930s by a local schoolteacher. The award-winning visitor centre at Ballycastle, open from Easter until the end of October, has a viewing platform looking out over the cliffs.

Céide Fields
The visitor centre.

The North Mayo Sculpture Trails

Tír Sáile is the largest public arts project ever undertaken in Ireland. It was inaugurated in 1993, during the Mayo 5000 celebrations. Fifteen mixed media sculptures were commissioned for installation along the coast from the southern tip of the Erris Peninsula to the Moy Estuary.

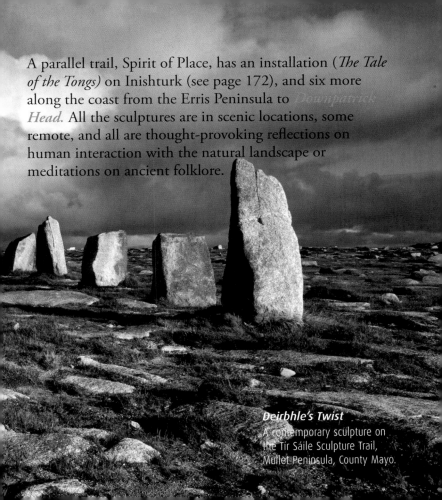

A parallel trail, Spirit of Place, has an installation (*The Tale of the Tongs*) on Inishturk (see page 172), and six more along the coast from the Erris Peninsula to *Downpatrick Head*. All the sculptures are in scenic locations, some remote, and all are thought-provoking reflections on human interaction with the natural landscape or meditations on ancient folklore.

Deirbhle's Twist
A contemporary sculpture on the Tír Sáile Sculpture Trail, Mullet Peninsula, County Mayo.

On the way to Downpatrick Head you will pass the Doonfeeny Standing Stone, believed to date from the Bronze Age. At five metres high, it is one of the tallest standing stones in Ireland.

Downpatrick Head is a very windy spot where you need to be careful not to get too close to the edge, although the views are amazing. Lying just off the head is the Dún Briste sea stack, once connected to the headland by a sea arch. During the Second World War there was a lookout on the head to deter any enemy vessels that might have strayed into Irish waters.

As you approach the town of Killala look out for the round tower, the last remnant of a monastery said to have been founded by St Patrick.

Killala has earned its place in Irish history. During the 1798 Rebellion General Humbert of France landed at *Killala Bay* and took the town for the rebels before winning a victory at Castlebar. The rebellion was soon crushed, however, Humbert was taken prisoner and Killala was recaptured by the British forces. Just off the road from Killala to Ballina, Moyne Friary and Rosskerk Friary are outstanding examples of late medieval abbeys. Moyne dates from the mid-15th century and was one of the biggest Franciscan abbeys in Ireland. The extensive buildings include magnificent, well-preserved cloisters. Moyne has a bloody history at English hands, and the monastery and its lands were eventually granted by Elizabeth I to Edward Barrett in the late 16th century. A small Franciscan community remained at the abbey until the end of the 18th century. The well-preserved abbey at Rosskerk was built in the mid-15th century on an estuary of the River Moy, for the Third Order of Franciscans.

Moyne Abbey

SS *Crete Boom*
Built in Shoreham in the UK in 1919.

Ballina, a port on the mouth of the River Moy, is the largest town in Mayo and has a couple of unique attractions. The SS *Crete Boom*, a ship made of concrete, has a permanent berth on the west bank of the river, monument to a brief flirtation with concrete ships that ended when the running costs proved

prohibitive. The Jackie Clarke Collection, housed in the old Provincial Bank building, is a collection of more than 10,000 documents and artefacts related to the struggle for Irish independence.

A grisly tale is attached to the megalithic dolmen just outside the town on Primrose Hill, known as the Dolmen of the Four Maols. The four Maols were brothers of noble birth who were lured into a plot to kill their foster brother, Ceallach, bishop of Kilmoremoy (present-day Ballina). They were arrested and executed, but their noble lineage meant that they were entitled to a proper burial, and they were interred at the dolmen that now bears their name.

Ballina
Aerial view of the town.

Dolmen of the Four Maols
Situated on Primrose Hill, overlooking the River Moy.

CHAPTER 8 The Surf Coast

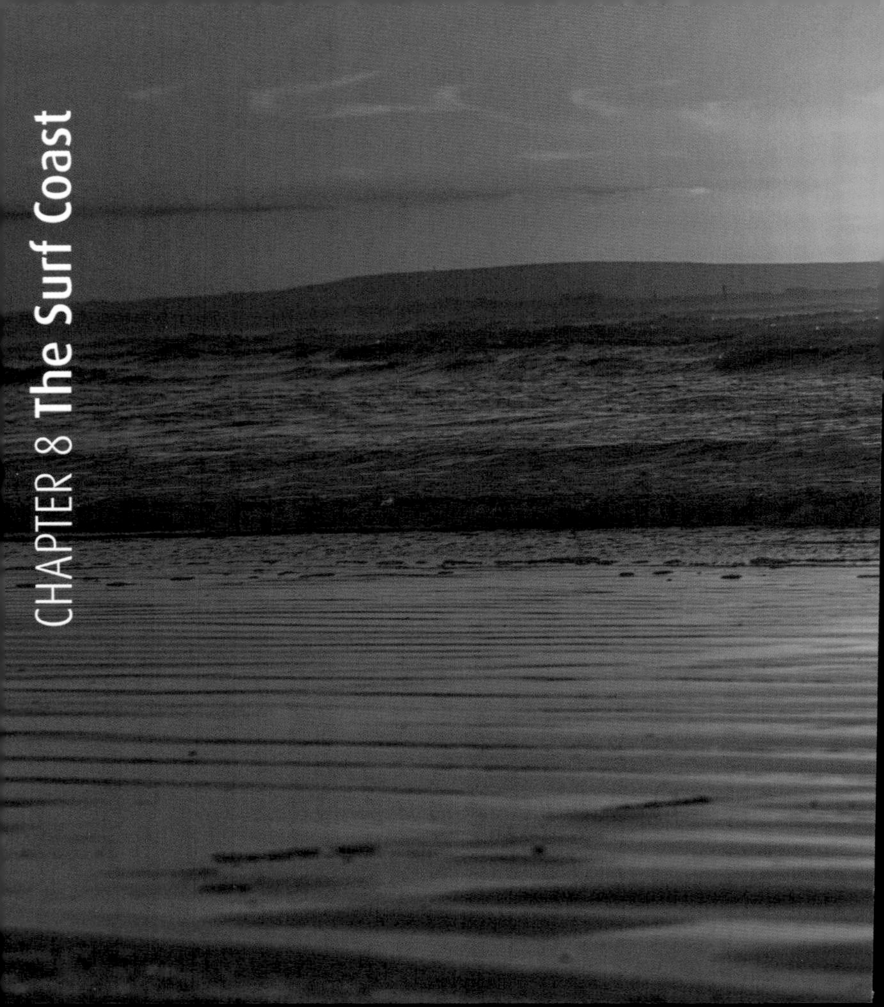

Sunset at Enniscrone

What to look out for along the way.

Key towns and villages
Enniscrone
Strandhill
Sligo
Mullaghmore

Viewing Points
Aughris Head; Mullaghmore
Head; Knocknarea Hill;
Deerpark Court Tomb; Connors
Island

Beaches
Easky; Dunmoran Strand;
Culleenamore Beach; Rosses
Point; Streedagh Beach;
Mullaghmore

Monuments
Easkey Castle; Carrowmore
passage tombs; Lissadell
House; Birthing Stone and
Beehive Huts (St Molaise's
monastery) Inishmurray; Sligo
Abbey; Creevykeel Court Tomb;
the Split Stone

Garden
Lissadell

Walks
Strandhill Loop Walk; Raghly Walk; Queen Maeve's Trail; Mullaghmore Headland Loop; Ballycroy Trail; Hazelwood Demesne Walks; the Rosses Walk

Offshore Islands
Coney Island; Inishmurray Island

Music
Cos Cos Sean Nós Festival (May); Wild Atlantic Sea Shanty Festival (June); Sligo Live (October)

Don't Miss!
The Fairy Glen; Glencar Waterfall; Rineen Woods; Lough Gill; Ben Bulben; Ballycroy National Park; Drumcliff graveyard; The Bullance Stone

Leaving Ballina and travelling up the coast of Sligo, you'll arrive at the lively seaside town of *Enniscrone*, with its five-kilometre stretch of sandy Blue Flag beach backed by sand dunes. It's a popular holiday destination and a good beginner surfers' destination. It's considered by some to enjoy better sunsets than elsewhere along this coast.

The next stop on the route is *Easkey*, a typical Irish seaside village that is internationally recognised as a surfers' paradise – it has two reef breaks, which produce the fast, hollow waves that are ideal for experienced surfers. If you're there around Halloween, don't miss the Easkey Scarecrow Festival.

Easkey Castle (also known as Roslee Castle), beside the

pier, is one of Ireland's earlier tower houses. It was built in 1207 by Oliver McDonnell, a Scottish Lord of the Isles who married into the O'Dowd clan. It was granted to a Williamite soldier in the late 17th century.

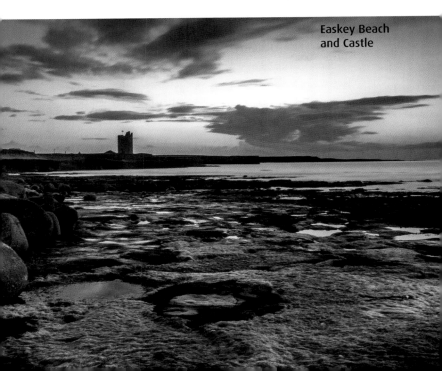

Easkey Beach and Castle

Split Stone

Ice Age boulder at Easkey.

Easkey Bridge, built in 1847 to replace an older bridge, leads out of the village towards Sligo. A drinking trough built into its wall, the 'Bullance Stone', contains water that has a reputation for curing skin infections.

Just outside Easkey on the road to Sligo there is a strange Ice Age boulder known as the Split Stone, said to have been divided vertically during an argument between Fionn Mac Cumhaill and another giant. There is a legend that anyone who walks through the split three times will be squashed by the stone closing over.

Aughris Head has the highest cliffs in Sligo with wonderful views, as well as an Iron Age promontory fort gradually being claimed by the sea. There is a trail to Dunmoran Strand, a remote and beautiful sandy beach.

A little further on, the Fairy Glen lives up to its name as a magical place. A narrow canyon that is difficult to find, its high limestone walls and lush vegetation close off the view of the sky, and the atmosphere along its one-kilometre length is damp and tropical.

Strandhill is a small seaside village with a dangerous beach that is a draw for experienced surfers. There is a seven-kilometre signposted loop walk from the beach, if you feel like stretching your legs and taking in the scenery. If you want a swim, Culleenamore Beach, just south of the village, is sandy and safe, and you might catch a glimpse of one of Ireland's largest seal colonies basking on the sandbanks. Strandhill is also home to the Voya Seaweed Baths, a great place for a spa treatment and a therapeutic seaweed bath.

At first sight Knocknarea Hill, slightly south of Strandhill, looks like a huge flat-topped boulder. Queen Maeve's Trail is a short 2.4-kilometre walk to the summit, from where you will get one of your first views of Ben Bulben, the iconic flat-topped mountain that dominates much of the scenery in this part of the Sligo coast. Legend has it that the large stone cairn on the top of Knocknarea is the tomb of Queen Maeve, who was buried standing up, wearing her armour and facing her enemies.

The Lore and Legends of Ben Bulben

Sometimes referred to as 'Ireland's Table Mountain', this distinctive flat-topped rock in the Dartry Mountains was formed during the last Ice Age, when retreating glaciers carved the earth into some strange formations. Its summit is home to a wide variety of flora and fauna. As well as providing inspiration for W. B. Yeats, who had a view of Ben Bulben from his childhood home, the mountain is connected with several Irish legends.

Ben Bulben was said to be one of the Fianna's preferred hunting grounds, and it was here that Fionn Mac Cumhaill met his beloved wife Sadhbh, who had been turned into

a deer by an evil druid. The story ended badly when the druid tricked Sadhbh into returning to the mountain with him and Fionn never saw her again. However, one day, while out hunting, he came across a fawn – this was his son, Oisín, who became one of the most famous heroes of the Fianna. Diarmuid and Gráinne are said to have sought refuge on the mountain from the ageing Fionn, who was betrothed to Gráinne.

Ben Bulben is said to be the only place where fairies can be seen by mortals – when their 'fairy door' into the mountain is open, good weather is on its way.

There are also historical associations – St Columba's famous Battle of the Books is said to have been fought on the slopes of the mountain in AD 560.

Just west of Sligo town is the Carrowmore passage tomb site, which has more tombs than any other Neolithic site in Ireland. Over 60 have been excavated here and one of them, Listoghil, has some megalithic carvings.

Carrowmore Tomb

Sligo, the coastal county town of Sligo, was founded in the early medieval period. It was given a royal charter in 1290; by the 15th century, as a result of this mark of royal favour, it had prospered. It was the port of departure for more than 30,000 emigrants during the Great Famine in the mid-19th century, a tragedy memorialised by a bronze sculpture on the quays. The town developed into a busy port and commercial centre in the late 19th century – this is when much of the town centre was built.

The ruin of Sligo Abbey, a Dominican foundation dating from the mid-13th century, is the only remaining medieval structure in the town.

Sligo has strong associations with the poet W. B. Yeats, and the Yeats International Summer School is held here in July and August each year (you will be reminded everywhere you go that this part of Sligo is Yeats country – his 'land of heart's desire'). Tread Softly, held in July, is an exploration of the relationship between the poet and his brother, the painter Jack B. Yeats. Sligo has a long tradition of music, honoured by the Cos Cos Sean Nós Festival in May, the unusual Wild Atlantic Sea Shanty Festival in June, and Sligo Live in October.

In a beautiful woodland setting, Lough Gill is a lovely place to while away a few hours, with plenty of walking, cycling and picnicking opportunities. One of the islands on the lake was the inspiration for Yeats's poem, 'The Lake Isle of Inisfree'. There are boat tours of the lake from the quays at the east of Sligo town. A short trail from the quays leads to a viewing point at Dooney Rock. You can have a lovely woodland stroll through Hazelwood Demesne, on the western shore of Lough Gill, following the sculpture trail through the forest.

Romantic Glencar Waterfall, just to the north of Lough Gill, is 11 kilometres west of Manorhamilton in County Leitrim.

Rosses Point
Sunset over the 17th hole at the golf course.

W. B. Yeats mentions it in his poem 'The Stolen Child'.

About eight kilometres outside Sligo town, Deerpark Court Tomb, a Neolithic burial place dating from the third millennium BC, is an atmospheric spot from which to enjoy great views over the Glencar Valley and Lough Gill.

Rosses Point is a Blue Flag beach resort at the entrance to Sligo Harbour. A monument to those lost at sea, *Waiting on Shore,* is a poignant reminder of the reality of life for people in these parts in years gone by. You can take a boat from Rosses Point to Coney Island, or drive over the five-kilometre causeway, Cummeen Strand, at low tide. There are few distractions on the island apart from beautiful scenery and sandy beaches – and one pub. The Rosses Walk is an easy stroll along the shoreline from the beach. Keep an eye out for the Metal Man beacon, pointing his finger in the direction of the treacherous rocks.

Lissadell House, constructed in the early 19th century, was the childhood home of the suffragette Eva Gore-Booth and her sister Constance Markievicz, one of the leaders of the 1916 Rising and the first female MP elected to the House of Commons at Westminster. The house was one of W. B. Yeats's haunts. There is an interesting guided tour of part of the house and the fee includes access to the wonderful walled Alpine and kitchen gardens. From Lissadell you can drive to Raghly Harbour to do the short loop that was a one of Yeats's favourite walks.

Lissadell House

Constance Markievicz
Sketch by W. B. Yeats.

St Colmcille founded a monastery at Drumcliff, between Ben Bulben and Drumcliff Bay, in AD 574. Records indicate that the round tower was hit by lightning at the end of the 14th century and only a portion is still standing. There is an exquisitely carved high cross, dating from the end of the first millennium AD. The graveyard of St Columba's Church at Drumcliff is the final burial place of W. B. Yeats.

Streedagh beach is a long sandy stretch backed by sand dunes and is popular with surfers. The three-kilometre walk to Connors Island will be rewarded with beautiful views. It's such a peaceful spot that it's hard to imagine that three ships from the Spanish Armada were wrecked here in 1588, with the loss of 1,600 men.

Inishmurray Island, to the north-west of Streedagh, is a wildlife sanctuary. The sixth-century settlement founded there by St Molaise is one of Ireland's best preserved monastic sites. The intact beehive hut and a birthing stone (used in rituals connected with fertility and childbirth) are remarkable. The island was attacked on several occasions by the Vikings and the monks eventually decided to relocate to the mainland in the ninth century. Inishmurray was inhabited until 1948 – the inhabitants were renowned for their very fine poitín, frequently smuggled to the mainland. There are boat trips out to Inishmurry from Mullaghmore Harbour.

Mullaghmore Head is one of the best surfing destinations in Europe and is a venue for international surfing competitions. The village of the same name is small and welcoming and has a lovely sandy beach. There is a four-kilometre loop walk around the headland, with stunning views out to sea and back towards the fairytale castle profile of Classiebawn.

Creevykeel Court Tomb, just north of the village of Cliffony, is one of the best examples in Ireland of a Neolithic court tomb. It was excavated in 1935, and it was clearly used throughout history for domestic and other purposes far removed from the builders' original intent.

Creevykeel Court Tomb

CHAPTER 9 The North-West Headlands

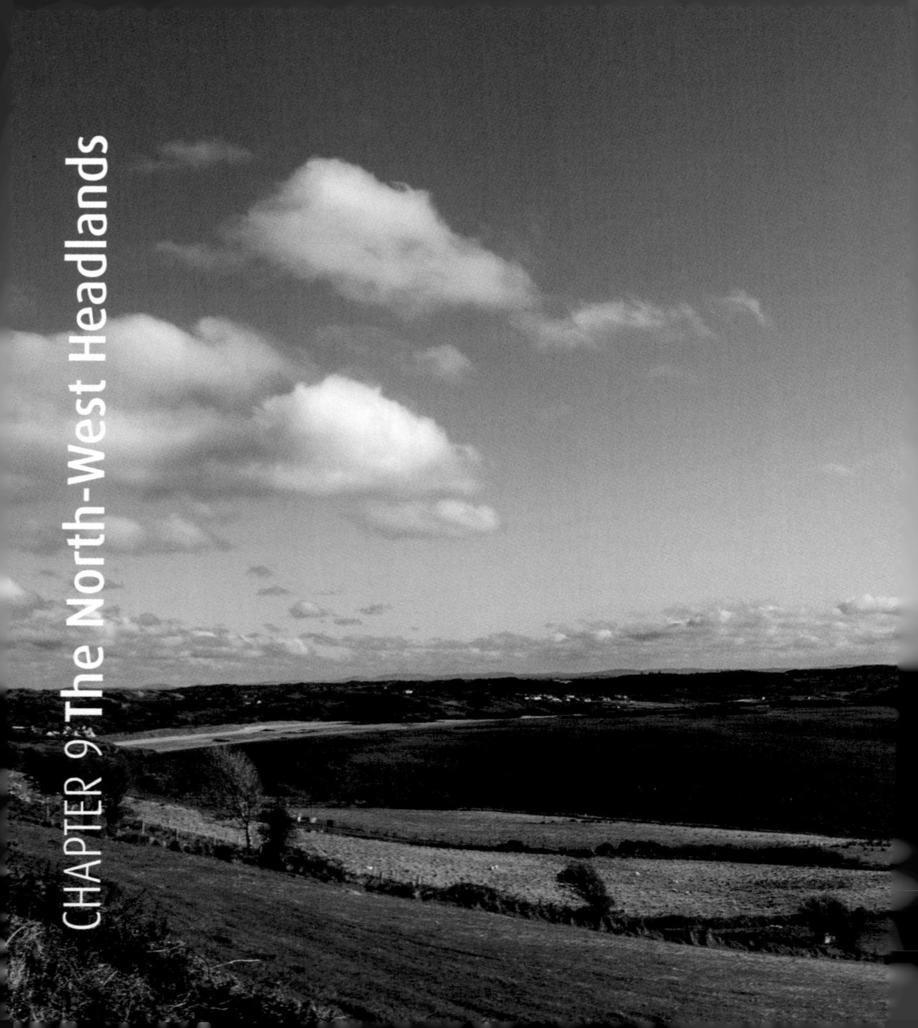

Panoramic view of Donegal
Bay and Fintra Beach

CHAPTER 9 Donegal Bay to Bunbeg

What to look out for along the way.

Key towns and villages
Bundoran
Ballyshannon
Donegal
Killybegs
Dungloe
Burtonport
Ardara
Bunbeg

Viewing Points
The Wishing Chair; St John's Point; Muckross Head; Slieve League; Malin Beg; Malin Bay; Port; Glengesh Pass; Crohy Head

Beaches
Bundoran; Tullan Strand; Rossknowlagh Beach; Murvagh Beach; Fintragh Bay; Silver Strand; Naran Beach; Carrickfinn Beach

Monuments
Kilbarron Castle; Kilclooney Dolmen; Donegal Castle

Gardens
Salthill Garden, Mountcharles

Walks
Roughey Walk; Bonny Glen Wood Loops

Offshore Islands
Arranmore; Owey Island; Cruit Island; Rathlin O'Birne Island

Food and drink
A Taste of Donegal (August); Wild Atlantic Craft Beer Festival, Bundoran (August)

Music
Sea Sessions Surf & Music Festival, Bundoran (June); Rory Gallagher International Tribute Festival, Bundoran (May/June); Mary from Dungloe Festival (July); Swell Fest, Arranmore (July); Ballyshannon Folk and Traditional Music Festival (August)

Don't Miss!
The Fairy Bridges
Glencolmkille Folk Village
Assarnacally Waterfall
Cara na Mara
Crohy Head
Slieve League Visitor Centre

The first stretch of the Donegal coast, just over the county border with Leitrim, is famous for its beaches, particularly the long sandy stretch at Bundoran, now a Blue Flag beach. A favourite holiday resort of generations of Irish families, Bundoran became popular in the late 18th century when Viscount Enniskillen built a holiday home there – it became such a mecca for wealthy holidaymakers that it was known for a time as 'the Brighton of Ireland'. These days it's still a popular holiday destination, and early birds can enjoy the Sea Sessions Surf and Musical Festival in May.

The beach of Tullan Strand is now an internationally popular surfing destination and has made Bundoran the Surf Capital of Ireland. It is also a great place for swimming and the main beach can get very crowded in the

Surfer William Alotti

During Expression Session, part of the annual Sea Sessions Surf and Musical Festival in Bundoran.

Tullan Strand
One of Donegal's renowned surf beaches.

summer months. If you prefer to get away from the beach, there are two good saltwater pools, West End Pool, and the Thruppenny (or Horse) Pool. Do check on the tides before using either pool.

You can get to Tullan from the town along the Roughey Walk, a scenic paved route that gives 360° views over Donegal Bay, from Ben Bulben in Sligo to Slieve League on the Donegal coast. Keep an eye out for the Fairy Bridges (there are no guard rails along the cliffs, so this part of the walk is best avoided if you have small children), ancient sea stacks that were the main tourist attraction in Bundoran in the 18th century and believed by the locals to have been haunted by fairies. In 1944 a visitor's guide to Bundoran included a little ditty about the sea stacks that give an indication of the atmosphere there:

The Fairy Bridges where the sprites
In moonlit splendour sport and play,
Span chasms dark and lowering where
The lashing waters dash and spray.

A second verse recommends visitors to try their luck at the Wishing Chair, said to have been carved out of a standing stone that marked the grave of an O'Flaherty chieftain.

And then the dear old Wishing Chair,
Where heartsick maids petitions lay,
Where thousands found each wish come true,
And ever bless the 'happy day'.

Your wish must be made in silence and never revealed, and it's recommended to tap the chair twice before getting up to signify that your wish is genuine. Legend aside, the views from the chair are stupendous.

Ballyshannon, on the River Erne, is one of the oldest towns in Ireland, having received a royal charter in

The Fairy Bridges

1613. The river was once spanned by a beautiful 14-arch bridge, replaced in 1946 by a single-arch bridge.

Ballyshannon has had a few famous sons: the poet William Allingham; the richest man in Ireland, William Connolly, Speaker of the Irish House of Commons; and the musician and songwriter Rory Gallagher, whose statue stands in the middle of the town. The Rory Gallagher International Tribute Festival brings 10,000 visitors to the town every May. It's not the only musical event in Ballyshannon, which has always had a strong musical tradition and hosts the Ballyshannon Folk and Traditional Music Festival each August, now running in tandem with the Wild Atlantic Craft Beer Festival.

Rory Gallagher
Statue in Ballyshannon.

Leaving Ballyshannon and heading north, you will see the sad ruins of Kilbarron Castle, built right at the edge of the cliffs in the 13th century. It was the home of the O'Clerys, advisers to the O'Donnell chieftains. Michael O'Clery is credited with the authorship of much of the Annals of the Four Masters. After the defeat of the O'Donnells at the Battle of Kinsale in 1601 and their subsequent flight to the continent, the O'Clerys had to surrender Kilbarron during the subsequent Plantation of Ulster. The castle, neglected, fell into ruin, and is in such a precarious condition that it's not possible to get close to it. However, a walk from Creevy Pier will give you a good view of the castle from a safe distance.

Continuing along the route of the Wild Atlantic Way you will come to the wide expanse of *Rossknowlagh*, a very popular Blue Flag beach that is good for both swimming and surfing. Although *Murvagh*, a little further north,

Rossknowlagh Beach

is also a Blue Flag beach, it is very exposed – if you're planning to spend some time there, stick close to the dunes that back it.

Donegal town, situated at the mouth of the River Eske, was used by the Vikings as a port after they invaded the town in the eighth century. They built a fort there, probably on the site of Donegal Castle – Dún na nGall means 'fort of the foreigners'. A good vantage point on the town can be had on a waterbus tour from Donegal Harbour (departures dependent on the tides), the highlight of which is a chance to see the Donegal Bay seal colony. If you visit Donegal during the last weekend in August, you will be able to enjoy a whole range of food-focused events at the Taste of Donegal festival.

Donegal Castle

Donegal Castle, an O'Donnell stronghold, was built at different times, but the oldest part, the O'Donnell Tower, is believed to have been constructed in the second half of the 15th century. The last O'Donnell to live in the castle was 'Red' Hugh, who died in Spain in 1602, having fled Ireland after the Battle of Kinsale the previous year. The castle was granted to Sir Basil Brooke in 1616. He undertook an extensive renovation, much of which can still be seen today. After the castle was abandoned in the 18th century it became dilapidated. It was taken over by the state in the late 19th century and the detailed restoration that was undertaken makes it an interesting place to visit.

Travelling west from Donegal, the 100-year-old walled gardens in the Salthill Demesne are about 200 metres from the sea near Mountcharles. The gardens have been redesigned to showcase a colourful selection of shrubs, plants and vegetables. They're open in the afternoons (except Sundays) from the beginning of May to the end of September.

A quick detour off the route as you travel along the north side of Donegal Bay is St John's Point, a long, narrow peninsula, the far end of which is an excellent place from which to enjoy the views. The cut-granite lighthouse on St John's Point came into operation in 1831, having been requested by the traders of Killybegs. It is now fully automated and the two lightkeepers' cottages have been converted to tourist accommodation.

Colourful Killybegs, with its natural deep-water harbour, is the largest fishing port in Ireland. In the past it was famous for its Donegal carpets, produced on the largest carpet loom in the world, and in demand internationally for state buildings such as the White House and Buckingham Palace. The factory closed in 2003, but in 2006 it was reopened as a heritage centre, providing information on Killybegs's maritime and carpet-making history. Guided tours include the chance to try out a ship simulator.

St John's Point
Lighthouse

Just outside Killybegs is the long sandy Blue Flag beach of *Fintragh Bay*, famous locally as the crash site of a US Air Force Flying Fortress bomber on 20 February 1944. A few kilometres further west, *Muckross Head* juts out into the sea, cliffs falling to either side. It overlooks a sandy beach, which looks idyllic but has dangerous rip tides.

Slieve League Cliffs

The Slieve League Cliffs are one of the most spectacular sights on the entire route of the Wild Atlantic Way, with the tallest summit, *Slieve League*, rising 600 metres out of the sea. The walk to the cliffs gives wonderful views across to the Sligo mountains. The cliffs have associations with St Brendan and were a place of pilgrimage for over a thousand years. A Napoleonic signal tower was sited on the cliffs, and the remains can still be seen.

The climb to the summit of Slieve League is only for the experienced and the Pilgrim's Path along the cliffs is sometimes difficult. One of the best ways to see the cliffs is from the water; you can book a trip at Teelin Harbour. You can learn about the history and importance of the cliffs at the Slieve League Visitor Centre at Teelin.

At the far end of the Slieve League Cliffs is the tiny village of *Malin Beg*, famous for its beautiful horseshoe-shaped beach, the aptly named Silver Strand. You can walk from the harbour to the old watchtower at Malin Bay for great views along the Slieve League Cliffs and across to Rathlin O'Birne Island, home to Ireland's first and only nuclear-powered lighthouse. An isotope generator was installed in 1974, but was replaced by a wind generator in 1987 and was switched over to solar power in 1991.

Rounding the corner of the peninsula you will come to Glen Bay and the small village of Glencolmcille, gateway to some of Donegal's most interesting landscapes and history. As its name suggests, the area has strong associations with St Colmcille, said to have battled with demons here. His feastday, 9 June, became a day of pilgrimage, and you can still follow the 15 stone markers along the three-hour route to a holy well. There is also a 10-kilometre signposted loop walk from the village.

The population of this area was greatly reduced by emigration during the 1950s, and in 1967 a local priest, Father McDyer, established a living history museum in a cluster of small cottages to show how people lived in the area. The museum provides a fascinating insight into life here in the 18th, 19th and 20th centuries.

The Wild Atlantic Way now goes inland along the road from Glencolmcille to Ardara through the breathtakingly beautiful Glengesh Valley. Travelling along the road from Ardara to the long, long Blue Flag *Naran Beach* (also known as Tramore) at Portnoo, you will see the iconic Kilclooney Dolmen, silhouetted against the sky. It is said to be one of Ireland's finest examples of a portal tomb. Information is available from the nearby Dolmen Centre in Naran and Portnoo.

Kilclooney Dolmen

If you head north from Glencolmcille, rather than taking the *Glengesh Pass*, you will come to Port. This was once a fishing village, but became deserted during the Great Famine. The waters of the cliff-lined cove reveal jagged rocks that have been formed by the wild Atlantic waves crashing against the shore. A little further to the north-east is Maghera, a stunning white beach with some tidal caves that can be explored at low tide. The beach has very strong currents, making it dangerous for swimming. The road from Maghera to Ardara passes the picturesque multi-levelled Assarnacally Waterfall.

The Bonny Glen Wood is a mixed forest and is a lovely place for a peaceful walk and a picnic – there are two loop walks around the lakes, where you will have the opportunity to see plenty of wildlife.

On the road to Dungloe, head west to the coast for Crohy Head on the Mullaghmullan Peninsula to see the strange rock formations, including the sea arch known as the 'Breeches'.

Dungloe is a small town most famous for its Mary from Dungloe Festival, held at the end of July each year, which attracts visitors from throughout the Irish diaspora. The singer Daniel O'Donnell was born in nearby Kincaslagh, and there is a visitor centre dedicated to him in Dungloe.

Burtonport, a long-established fishing village, is the departure point for ferries to the island of *Arranmore*.

Bonny Glen Waterfall

There are several crossings daily and the journey is short, about 15 minutes. The largest island in Donegal, Arranmore, has been inhabited since prehistoric times and has a vibrant heritage and cultural life. The exposed west coast of the island has spectacular cliffs that are home to a variety of seabirds, while the sheltered southern and eastern shores have sandy beaches that are perfect for swimming. There are plenty of waymarked trails across the island. Arranmore has a good reputation for traditional Irish music, and visitors at the end of July can enjoy the Swell Fest music and arts festival.

A little further up the mainland coast, just north of the village of Kincaslagh, there are two more islands. A small bridge connects Cruit to the mainland. There are lots of sandy beaches and plenty of opportunities for rock-climbing on the granite cliffs. Tiny Owey Island, just off

The bridge to Cruit

Owey Island
Rock climber on the eastern shore of Owey Island.

Cruit, has a few permanent residents, who live completely off grid – electricity was never brought out to the island and there is no mains water supply. Transport to the island from Cruit can be arranged. If you enjoy rock-climbing and sea kayaking and don't mind living off grid for a while, Owey is the ideal destination.

The small headland of **Carrickfinn** is home to Donegal Airport, twice voted the airport with the most scenic approach in the world. The headland is dotted with small beaches and coves, but the most popular is the glorious Blue Flag beach beside the airport runway.

The tiny village of **Bunbeg** is a ferry departure point for Tory Island (see page 240). Look out for the remains of the *Cara na Mara* on the beach. It was wrecked in the 1970s and has become something of an attraction, known in the locality as 'Bád Eddie', or 'Eddie's Boat'.

Eddie's Boat

The beach at
Carrickfinn

CHAPTER 10 The Northern Peninsulas

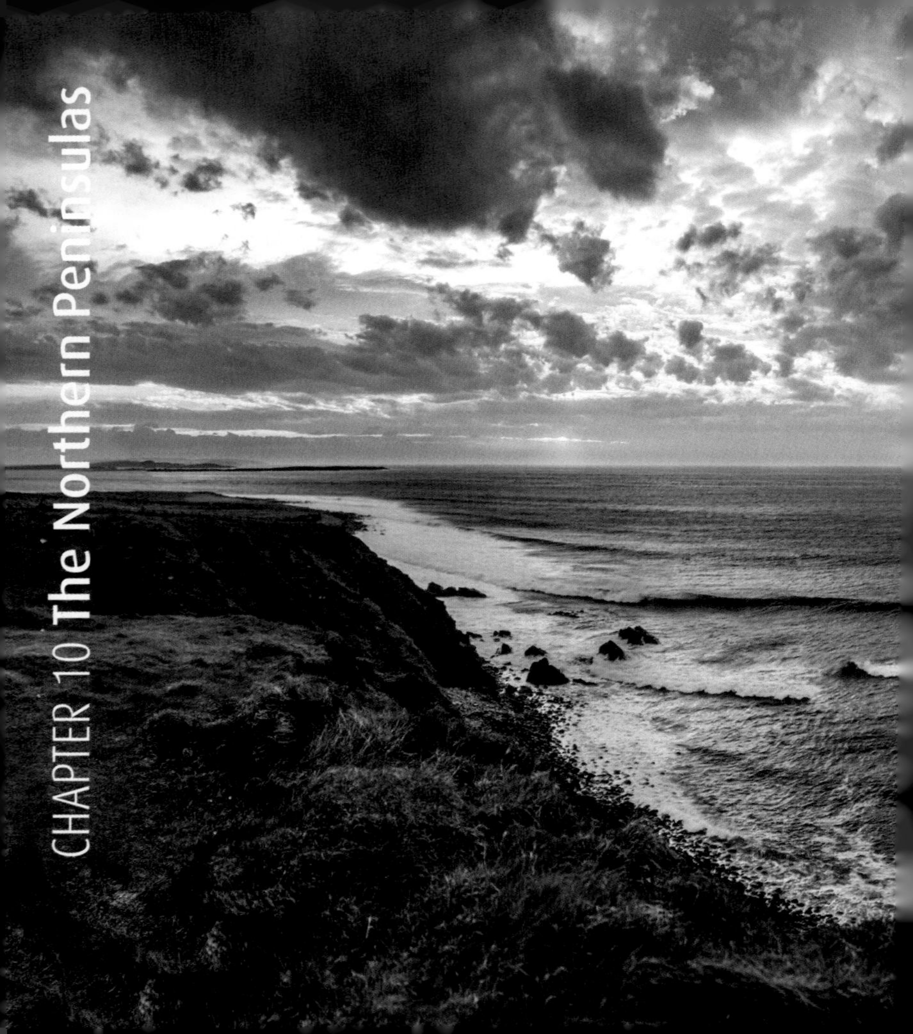

Bloody Foreland coastline

What to look out for along the way.

Key towns and villages
Dunfanaghy
Carrigart
Letterkenny
Buncrana

Viewing Points
Bloody Foreland; Horn Head;
Rosguill Peninsula; Lough
Kinny; Fanad Head; Dunree
Head; Mamore Gap; Malin
Head; Magilligan Point View;
Inishowen Head; Banba's Crown

Beaches
Marblehill Beach; Sheephaven
Bay; Downings Beach; Dooagh;
Boyeeghter Bay; Doaghmore
Strand; Ballymastocker Bay;
Lenan Beach; Tullagh Bay;
Pollan Bay; Five Fingers Strand;
Culdaff Beach; Kinnagoe Bay;
Stroove; Killahoey; Port Arthur
Beach; Stragill Strand; White
Strand; Lisfannon

Monuments
Doe Castle; Burt Castle; Grianán
of Aileach; Fort Dunree;
Carrickabraghy Castle

Garden
Carrablagh House, Portsalon

 Walks
Ards Forest Park Walks; Inch Island; Inishowen Head Loop

 Offshore Islands
Tory Island; Inishbofin, Inch

 Music
O'Flaherty's OTB, Buncrana (July)

 Don't Miss!
Bloody Foreland sunset
Glenveagh National Park
The Bridge of Tears
McSwyne's Gun
Great Pollet Arch
Lough Swilly
Doagh Famine Village
Malin Well
Lough Foyle
Inch Wildlife Reserve
Glenevin Waterfall
Lenan Fort
Port-a-Doras
Tau Cross, Tory Island
Northern Lights
Flight of the Earls Heritage Centre

On the road from Bunbeg to the north-western tip of Donegal, against the background of the Glenveagh National Park, you will pass the lovely sandy stretch of Port Arthur Beach, seven kilometres south of the best sunsets you will encounter on the entire Wild Atlantic Way route. The Bloody Foreland gets its name from the colour of the cliffs as the sun sets. Even without a sunset, the views from here are amazing. It's a wonderfully craggy stretch of coast, littered with sea stacks and home to seabirds of all kinds, from gannets to puffins. You may be lucky enough to see dolphins and seals, and even the occasional whale.

From the *Bloody Foreland* you will be able to see *Tory Island*, the most remote inhabited island in Ireland. Even though it is only 14.5 kilometres off the coast, weather conditions dictate that it is a remote place, home to an independent population that has preserved its ancient customs and traditions – they even elect their own king, the Rí Thoraí. The rugged coast tells the tale of the wild Atlantic weather that buffets the island, shielding the islanders from all but the most determined invaders. The monks of St Colmcille's sixth-century monastery had the additional protection of a round tower to defend them from the Viking raids that were common. Despite the natural and built defences, the monastery was destroyed by English forces in the late 16th century and the monks fled to the mainland. An unusual artefact is the stone Tau cross, one of only two in Ireland (the other is in County Clare), suggesting that the monks had contact with the Coptic Christians of Egypt. The island is very small and is easily explored on foot or bicycle.

Tau Cross
Ancient link with Egypt.

Glenveagh National Park

The peace and tranquillity of the beautiful scenery of Glenveagh National Park, the second-largest national park in Ireland, is at odds with its cruel history. When the Neo-Gothic Glenveagh Castle was built by John Adair, he instigated one of the worst evictions in the 19th century, purely so that the poverty of his tenants would not blight the beauty of the castle's surroundings. A later owner, son of an Irish immigrant to the United States, gifted the castle

and grounds to the Irish state in 1979. The enormous park, which encompasses Mount Errigal and Slieve Sneacht, is a stunningly beautiful wildlife haven. On the road from the castle a bridge, known as the 'Bridge of Tears', commemorates those evicted by Adair. It was the point at which the emigrants parted for the last time from their loved ones on the way to the ships that would take them to the New World.

You can take a ferry to the island from the pier at Bunbeg (see page 234), or from Magheroarty, west of the Bloody Foreland. Magheroarty has a beautiful crescent-shaped Green Coast beach with white sand that looks pink in certain light.

The drive along this part of the route is all about the views, and the best of them can be had from *Horn Head*. The route does a loop around the headland from the village of Dunfanaghy in Sheephaven Bay. The sheer vertical drop of the cliffs provides a safe breeding ground for many varieties of seabird. There are the remains of two watchtowers on the headland, one Napoleonic, the other dating from the

Second World War. On wild days, the blowhole known as McSwyne's Gun on the western side of the peninsula gives a spectacular display, forcing water high into the air, with sound effects to match. Keep your distance, as stones and other debris are sometimes forced up too.

One of Donegal's most popular beaches is in Sheephaven Bay, east of Dunfanaghy. The sheltered Blue Flag beach of Marblehill is fringed by trees and sand dunes. Even if it's not swimming weather, it's a lovely place for a stroll. The Blue Flag beach at Killahoey is a quiet spot for a swim.

Magheroarty Beach

Doe Castle, on the last western promontory as you work your way around Sheephaven Bay, is very strategically located, bounded by the sea on three sides and on the fourth by a sea-filled moat. It is first mentioned in 1544, but it is likely to be at least a century older. It looks slightly different from the usual Irish tower house – it was the stronghold of a Scottish mercenary clan, the MacSweeneys, and it has the appearance of a defensive tower in Scotland. The impressive bawn wall was a later addition. Guided tours of the castle's interior are available.

Ards Forest Park, generally

Doe Castle

regarded as one of the most beautiful and varied forest parks in the country, extends to the coast and is a good place for a walk. There are several signposted routes, varying in length from one to 13 kilometres. One of the walks takes you past a mass rock, used to celebrate mass outdoors during the Penal Days when the practice of Catholic rites was outlawed.

The *Rosguill Peninsula* has some of the most beautiful beaches in Donegal, many of which can be reached by taking the Atlantic Drive around the peninsula. Downings Beach is a Blue Flag beach and possibly the best one for swimming, while the beach at Melmore is spectacular but not very safe. Idyllic little Dooagh is very private. Wild Boyeeghter Bay, also known as the Murder Hole, is inaccessible by car, but is an impressive spot.

Doaghmore Strand on the western coast of the Fanad may be one of the least frequented beaches in the country, simply because people don't know about it. It's an enormous beach, well worth a visit. The remains of a ship wrecked on this peninsula can be seen, although it's almost completely buried in the sand on the upper reaches of the beach.

The Fanad Peninsula is unusual in that it has several freshwater lakes close to the seashore, the nicest of which is Lough Kinny. At the tip of the peninsula, *Fanad Head* has had a role in maritime safety for two centuries. The original lighthouse, which came into operation in 1811, was replaced in 1886. Several of the lighthouse buildings have been converted to tourist accommodation.

At the entrance to Lough Swilly, the Great Pollet Arch is a remarkable example of a sea arch. The best view is from the beach.

Although Lough Swilly is an unlikely place for a garden, Carrablagh in Portsalon was established in the middle of the 19th century, with many fine specimen plantings. These are protected from the harsh climate by the surrounding woodland. Opening times are limited to five Thursdays in May and June, but this delightful garden is worth visiting. The beautiful Blue Flag beach at *Ballymastocker Bay* stretches from Portsalon to the

**Fanad Head
Lighthouse**

Knockalla Hills. If you climb to the shoulder of the hills you will get a great view of the long stretch of strand.

En route to Letterkenny you will pass Rathmullan, where a Napoleonic watchtower now houses the Flight of the Earls Heritage Centre, open from June until the middle of September. It tells the story of the 1607 flight to the continent of Hugh O'Neill, Earl of Tyrone, and Rory

O'Donnell, Earl of Tyrconnell, the last of the great Irish chieftains. Their departure point, in a French ship, was Rathmullan. In the summer you can take a ferry from Buncrana across Lough Swilly to Rathmullan.

Letterkenny, on the River Swilly, is the biggest town in Donegal, straddling the Fanad and Inishowen Peninsulas. It was established in the 17th century during the Ulster Plantations. When Wolfe Tone landed at Lough Swilly in 1798 with a force of 3,000 French troops he was arrested and held at Letterkenny's Laird's Hotel.

Leaving Letterkenny and travelling north on the Inishowen Peninsula you will see the ruins of Burt Castle, outlined

Rathmullan Pier

against the sky on a hill overlooking Lough Swilly. Built in the mid-16th century as one of a network of O'Doherty strongholds on Inishowen, it was a substantial structure, a three-storey square tower with two round watchtowers, which would have given 360° views over the surrounding countryside. While you can't get to the top of the tower, the views from the hill on which it stands are just as good.

The Grianán of Aileach, the royal seat of the O'Neills, kings of Aileach, was built on Greenan Mountain with commanding views of the Rivers Foyle and Swilly. The site is imbued with mythology and history – it has links with the legendary Tuatha Dé Dannan and St Patrick. The fort was razed to the ground in AD 676, and its replacement was destroyed in 1101. In the 1870s the drystone walls of the circular fort were rebuilt by Bishop Walter Bernard of Derry. A series of internal terraces and steps will take you to the top of the walls to take in the breathtaking views.

South of Buncrana, the small island of *Inch*, an internationally important wildfowl reserve, is connected to the mainland by a causeway. There are three bird hides and several walking trails.

Buncrana is the largest town on Inishowen and is a popular holiday spot. It has several good beaches – Stragill Strand to the north of the town and the White Strand and *Lisfannon* to the south. The town hosts a two-day live music festival, O'Flaherty's OTB, early in July.

Fortifications were built on *Dunree Head* in the early 19th century as part of the Napoleonic coastal defences. A substantial fort was built in 1895 to guard the entrance to Lough Swilly. It was used as a lookout during the First World War, and Irish troops were stationed there during the Second World War to prevent any violation of Ireland's neutrality. Fort Dunree is now a military museum.

The *Mamore Gap*, a pass through the Urris Hills, offers sweeping views of the area and access to a holy well dedicated to St Eigne, an ancient pilgrimage site.

Not far from the Mamore Gap the mountains fall gently towards the coast. Lenan Beach is very secluded and rarely used. You will find the remains of a sizeable fort dating from 1895 on Lenan Head.

Tullagh Bay is a popular beach, ideal for horse-riding. When conditions are right, it's also good for surfing. Glenevin Waterfall, near Clonmany, is a great place for a stroll and a leisurely picnic.

Carrickabraghy Castle

Pollan Bay is a lovely beach on the Isle of Doagh (once an island but now joined to the mainland), popular with water sports enthusiasts, but is not very safe for swimming. The remains of Carrickabraghy Castle, a 16th-century O'Doherty stronghold, can be seen on a rocky outcrop at the end of the beach. An 1802 drawing by a Sir William Smith shows a far more complete structure, but the wild Atlantic weather since then has reduced the castle to a ruin that is in danger of collapse. Funds have been raised for its upkeep and restoration work is ongoing.

The Doagh Famine Village is an attractive museum of Irish life from the Great Famine to the present day. It's very family friendly, and the guides are exceptionally enthusiastic.

Although its not suitable for swimming because of strong currents, Five Fingers Strand is a wild and beautiful place for an energetic walk. There are five jagged sea stacks at one end, hence the name, and the beach is backed by some of the highest sand dunes in Europe.

Malin Head, right at the most northerly tip of the peninsula, is a wild place, and hundreds of ships have been wrecked on the rocks here. The highest point on the headland is a small hill known as Banba's Crown, after the legendary queen. This is the best vantage point and the site of a Napoleonic signal tower. The hill has poignant associations as the place where the families of emigrants to the New World waved their last farewell to their loved ones. Malin Head is one of the best places in Ireland to catch a sight of the Northern Lights, usually during the long dark nights between November and February.

Coming down from Malin Head on the north-eastern face of the peninsula, you will pass the Malin Well, a holy well and place of pilgrimage beside the ruins of a church. There are two popular beaches along this stretch, *Culdaff Beach* and *Kinnagoe Bay*. Both are good for swimming.

Inishowen Head is at the entrance to Lough Foyle. The best way to enjoy the panoramic views is by doing the eight-kilometre signposted loop walk around the head. A good starting point for the walk is Stroove, a very small but picturesque beach near Inishowen Head. It is overlooked by a lighthouse dating from 1837. You can also get to a strange rock formation from Stroove. Port-a-Doras is a natural doorway in a large rock on the shore, which would otherwise block the way.

Magilligan Point View gives wonderful views of Lough Foyle and across to the Martello tower at Magilligan Point in County Derry. The final stretch of the Wild Atlantic Way continues down the pleasant Lough Foyle coast, ending at the border with Northern Ireland.

Magilligan Point
On the other side of the border between Northern Ireland and the Republic of Ireland.

Picture credits

The publisher gratefully acknowledges the following image copyright holders. All images are copyright © individual rights holders unless stated otherwise. Every effort has been made to trace copyright holders, or copyright holders not mentioned here. If there have been any errors or omissions, the publisher would be happy to rectify this in any reprint.

Images labelled SS: Shutterstock
p1 Photoneye/SS
p3 Shawnwil23/SS
p4 Shutterupeire/SS
p9 Lukassek/SS
p9 Gabriel12/SS
p10 Jean Renaud/SS
p15 Everett Historical/SS
p15 Rudy Maree/SS
p16 Michael Diggin
p17 Ristic Sasha/SS
p19 Michael Diggin
p20 Michael Diggin
p21 Michael Collins/Wikipedia
p22 Michael Diggin
p22 Rezimov/SShutterstock
p23 Kieran Hayes/SS
p24 Tony Hall/Flickr
p25 Superbass/Wikipedia
p25 Geoffrey B Johnson Media/SS
p26 Timaldo/SS
p26 NLI/CC
p27 Wikipedia
p28 Creative Commons
p29 D Leeming69/SS
p30 Timaldo/SS
p31 Michael Diggin
p32 Michael Diggin
p33 Phil Darby/SS
p35 RR Photo/SS
p36 Stefano Valeri/SS
p38 Stefano Valeri/SS
p42 Fabiano's Photo/SS
p43 Sebastian Wasek/Alamy
p44 Gary Maccri/SS
p45 Philips Photos/SS
p46 Phil Darby/SS
p47 Pom Pom/SS
p47 Phil Darby/SS
p48 Archaeo Images/Alamy
p49 Timaldo/Alamy

p50 Philips Photos/SS
p51 Gráinne Watts
p52 Andrzej Bartyzel/SS
p52 Johannes Rigg/SS
p53 Corey Macri/SS
p54 Algiridas Gelazius
p55 Cori Macri/SS
p56 Joan Kruse/Alamy
p57 Design Pic Inc/Alamy
p58 Timaldo/SS
p59 Corey Macri/SS
p60 Ondrej Prochazka/SS
62 Michael David Murphy/Alamy
p65 PJ Photography/SS
p66 Louie Lea/SS
p70 Diak/SS
p71 Michael Diggin
p73 Steve Allen/SS
p74 Captblack76/SS
p75 Attila Jandi/SS
p76 Stefan Missing/SS
p79 M N Studio/SS
p80 Irene Lorenz/SS
p82 Everett Historical/SS
p84 Stephen Power/SS
p86 Paolo Trovo/SS
p87 Teapot Press
p89 Patryk Kosmider/SS
p91 Joe Dunkley/SS
p94 Gabriella Insuratelu/SS
p94 Nick Fox/SS
p96 Wikipedia
p97 Rolf G Wackenburg/SS
p98 Lyd Photography/SS
p99 Londubn/SS
p101 Noel O'Neil/SS
p103 StockWithMe/SS
p104 Stephen Long
p105 Atila Jandi/SS
p106 Kevin George/SS
p108 Colm K/SS
p109 Tigue O'Donoghue/SS
p110 Captback76/SS
p113 David Fitzell/SS

p114 David Fitzell/SS
p114 Heronimo Custodis/SS
p115 Gabriel 12/SS
p116 Shutterupeire/SS
p120 NLI/Flickr
p121 Library of Congress
p122 Wesley Cowpar/SS
p123 Wikipedia
p124 Lukasz Pajor/SS
p125 Joost van Uffelen/SS
p127 Johannes Rigg/SS
p128 JimJam194/SS
p129 Timaldo/SS
p131 Shutterupeire/SS
p132 Michael Diggin
p134 Patryk Kosmider/SS
p137 Lisandro Luis Trarbach/SS
p138 Anthony Patrick Saoud/SS
p142 Catherine Kronin/Flickr
p142 Andreas Riemenschneider/Flickr
p143 Xinhua/Alamy
p145 Mark Gusev/SS
p146 Stefano Valeri/SS
p148 Lorenz/Wikipedia
p149 Stefano Valeri/SS
p150 Wikipedia
p151 Jim 596/Wikipedia
p152 Rihardzz/SS
p154 A G Baxter/SS
p156 Teapot Press
p157 Lisandro Luis Trarbach/SS
p158 Louis-Michel Desert/SS
p161 Johannes Rigg/SS
p162 Bartkowski/SS
p164 Wikipedia
p164 Gabriela Insuratelu/SS
p165 DAJ Holmes/SS
p166 Bernd Meissner/SS
p171 Cynthia Shirk/SS

p171 PJ Photography/SS
p172 Sasapee/SS
p173 Michael McLaughlin
p174 David Lyons/Alamy
p175 Sandra Ramacher/SS
p176 Kriangkrai Thitmakorn/SS
p177 Michael Diggin
p177 Vincent MacNamara/SS
p178 Lisandro Luis Trarbach/SS
p180 Richard Semik/SS
p181 Gabriela Insuratelu/SS
p182 Colin Majury/SS
p183 Johannes Rigg/SS
p184 Lisandro Luis Trarbach/SS
p187 Susanne Pommer/SS
p188 DVLCom/SS
p190 Gareth McCormack/Alamy
p191 Ghotion/SS
p193 George Munday/Alamy
p195 Shawnwil23/SS
p196 Ak Photomadnes/SS
p196 Daniel Struk/SS
p197 Kinsella/Wikipedia
p198 Daniel Struk/SS
p203 Michel Seelen/SS
p204 Radharc Images/Alamy
p206 Nordic Moonlight/SS
p208 Jane McIlroy/SS
p210 Tim Murphy/SS
p211 NGI
p211 Nigel Aspdin/Wikipedia
p213 Milosz Maslanka/SS
p214 Ian Mitchinson/SS
p218 Rihardzz/SS
p219 MN Studio/SS
p220 MN Studio/SS
p221 Lukassek/SS
p222 Wikipedia
p223 Rob Crandall/SS

p225 Peter Crocka/SS
p226 Alexilina/SS
p229 Lukassek/SS
p231 Richard Wayman/Alamy
p232 Ian Mitchison/SS
p233 Gareth McCormack/Alamy
p234 Karel Cerny/SS
p235 Paul Shiels/SS
p236 Lukassek/SS
p241 Arco Images GmbH/Alamy
p242 Lyd Photographty/SS
p245 Design Pics Inc/Alamy
p246 Mark McColl/SS
p249 Madrugada Verde/SS
p250 Panda 17/SS
p253 Shawnwil23/SS
p255 Gordon Dunn/SS
FRONT COVER:
Alex Segre/Alamy
RR Photo/SS
Wlask Photos/SS
Patryk Kosmider/SS
Johannes Rigg/SS
Tony Potter
Tony Potter
Tony Potter
Shutterupeire/SS
Grafxart/SS
Joshua Hartmann/SS
Ghotion/SS
Tony Potter
Tony Potter
SPINE:
Johnny Griese/SS
BACK COVER:
Gabriel 12/SS
Tony Potter
Maria Janus/SS
Algirdas Gelazius/SS